ADVANCE PRAISE

A must-read guide that equips young people to build lasting financial stability and opportunity. This book breaks down essential financial concepts with clarity and compassion, giving students the knowledge and confidence they need to navigate college, work, and adulthood. It is a powerful resource for empowering the next generation to achieve economic mobility.

Dr. John B. King Jr., SUNY Chancellor & 10th U.S. Secretary of Education

The Student's Guide to Financial Freedom is the money playbook I wish I had in school. Paris makes building wealth feel simple, clear, and doable for every student.

Tiffany "The Budgetnista" Aliche, NYT-Bestselling Author of *Get Good With Money*

Paris Woods speaks directly to young people with honesty and heart, breaking down money in a way that feels practical and personal. This isn't another lecture about budgeting; it's a roadmap to real freedom, designed for students who want to live well and build wealth on their own terms.

Kiersten Saunders, Co-Host, rich & REGULAR Podcast

Opportunity shouldn't depend on zip code. *The Student's Guide to Financial Freedom* gives students the tools to build wealth early, make smart choices, and take control of their future. This book is a game-changer for creating equity and access.

CJ McCollum, NBA Player & Philanthropist

The Student's Guide to Financial Freedom helps young people demystify money and provides a helpful guide on how they can take control of their financial futures so they can lead, dream, and thrive.

Kwame Owusu-Kesse, CEO, Harlem Children's Zone, Co-founder, William Julius Wilson Institute at Harlem Children's Zone

Woods gives students something our education system too often denies them: accessible knowledge to avoid debt traps and begin building wealth before they even cross the graduation stage. Every student, educator, and parent committed to breaking cycles of economic extraction should read this book.

Dr. David J. Johns, CEO & Executive Director, National Black Justice Collective

Young people are paying the price for America's deeply inhumane approach to college financing. This new guide offers new perspectives on ways to traverse the current system, gaining the financial power—and hopefully the credentials—to get involved in changing it.

Dr. Sara Goldrick-Rab, teacher, author, scientist, and advocate

In today's society, our scholars are graduating without the skill set to be successful at adulting. *The Student's Guide to Financial Freedom* is a huge step in the right direction for all students to have access to the knowledge to build a financial foundation. Our culture needs this and our children need this guide!

Kimberly Neal-Brannum, Founder & Executive Director, BELIEVE Schools

In a world filled with distractions and misinformation, it is critical that students and prospective students have access to reliable and verifiable help for money management matters. There's no time like the present for individuals to avoid debt and build wealth with joy and hope. This book does just that!!!

Dr. Richard Rhodes, President, Texas A&M University

The Student's Guide to Financial Freedom cuts through financial complexity to give students the essential tools they need to avoid debt traps, build wealth early, and secure their financial future.

Trina Gary, Founder & Executive Director, Independent Trust

This guide is the gift every student needs—real talk about money, written in a way that actually makes sense. So many learn the hard way what Dr. Woods teaches here with clarity, compassion, and just a bit of tough love.

Michael A. Mallory, President & CEO, Ron Brown Scholar Program

At Education Leaders of Color, we work to end generational poverty and create opportunities for young people to determine their own destinies. *The Student's Guide to Financial Freedom* embodies that mission. It doesn't just teach young people how to manage money; it gives them a sense of agency and possibility. Every student deserves this roadmap to financial freedom.

Sharhonda Bossier, CEO, Education Leaders of Color

Young people tell us again and again that navigating personal finances is one of the most challenging parts of "adulting." *The Student's Guide to Financial Freedom* delivers clear, easy-to-follow steps for young people navigating major financial choices—empowering them to pursue the life they choose.

Cate Swinburn, Co-Founder & CEO, YouthForce NOLA

This is the book I wish I had as a high school student, and a book I'm grateful now exists for my children. Through the wisdom of her lived experiences and deep financial acumen, Paris Woods has written a relatable, empowering, illuminating guide for students on building wealth.

Idrissa Simmonds-Nastili, Executive Vice President, leadership coach, and author

As a professor who teaches personal finance to college students and the parent of two recent college graduates, I heartily endorse *The Student's Guide to Financial Freedom*. I recommend this book to every high school or college student who wants to take control of their money, make wiser financial choices, and ultimately achieve independence.

Jason Jimerson, Franklin College Professor, former insurance agent, and co-author of The Sociology of Money

Dr. Paris Woods shows students how to test drive their dreams, align their goals with identity and purpose, and step into adulthood with confidence and options. This is financial literacy as freedom, woven with equity, community, and the power to design a life on their own terms.

Keisha Scarlett, Ed.D., mother, national education leader and former superintendent

The Student's Guide to Financial Freedom is exactly what today's students need. Paris meets young people where they are and gives them the tools and confidence to build the future they deserve. Every high school and college student should read this book.

Chidi Asoluka, Founder & CEO, The NewComm Project

In my work, I see how financial literacy can change the course of a student's life almost instantly once they step foot on a college campus, from understanding their financial aid award letter to managing their refund check and even choosing a major. *The Student's Guide to Financial Freedom* breaks down these complex topics and makes them accessible, relatable, and actionable for students.

Clara Baron-Hyppolite, Executive Director, College Beyond

THE STUDENT'S GUIDE TO FINANCIAL FREEDOM

A Real-World Money Guide
to Help Young People Build Wealth,
Avoid Traps, and Plan for Freedom

Dr. Paris Woods

© 2026 Paris Woods

All rights reserved. No part of this publication may be reproduced, distributed, or transmitted in any form or by any means, including photocopying, recording, or other electronic or mechanical methods, without the prior written permission of the publisher, except in the case of brief quotations embodied in critical reviews and certain other noncommercial uses permitted by copyright law.

Although the author and publisher have made every effort to ensure that the information in this book was correct at press time, the author and publisher do not assume and hereby disclaim any liability to any party for any loss, damage, or disruption caused by errors or omissions, whether such errors or omissions result from negligence, accident, or any other cause.

Adherence to all applicable laws and regulations, including international, federal, state, and local governing professional licensing, business practices, advertising, and all other aspects of doing business in the US, Canada, or any other jurisdiction is the sole responsibility of the reader and consumer.

Neither the author nor the publisher assumes any responsibility or liability whatsoever on behalf of the consumer or reader of this material. Any perceived slight of any individual or organization is purely unintentional.

The resources in this book are provided for informational purposes only and should not be used to replace the specialized training and professional judgment of a licensed professional.

Neither the author nor the publisher can be held responsible for the use of the information provided within this book. Please always consult a trained professional before making any decision regarding your personal finance and investment decisions.

ISBN 978-1-7376066-2-8

Book Cover Design by ebooklaunch.com

Book Interior Design by Julie Karen Hodgins

For Jaiden, DeSean, and Clinton

**The young men in my life
whose journeys I cherish**

**and whose dreams I hope will be
realized beyond measure.**

CONTENTS

PREFACE	**10**
INTRODUCTION	**14**

PART I: HOW TO STAY OUT OF THE DEBT TRAP

CHAPTER 1: CREDIT — **20**
- Why So Many Adults Struggle with Debt — 22
- The Truth About Credit — 24
- The Minimum Payment Trap — 25
- Your Credit Score: Friend or Foe? — 28
- How to Build an Emergency Fund (Even on a Small Budget) — 29
- How to Use Credit Without Getting Trapped — 32

CHAPTER 2: CARS — **38**
- Will You Need a Car – and How to Decide — 40
- The Real Cost of a Car (And How to Avoid Getting Trapped) — 41
- How to Own a Car Without Going Broke — 45
- Why "Used" Doesn't Mean "Junk" — 45
- If You Can't Pay Cash Yet — 47
- My Car Story — 48

CHAPTER 3: EDUCATION — **52**
- Why Student Loans Can Be Risky — 56
- Step 1: Find the True Cost of School — 59
- Step 2: Match Yourself to Funding Sources — 61
- Step 3: Fill the Gap without Loans — 63
- Make Good Choices — 66
- What I Wish I Knew Earlier — 67

IF YOU ALREADY HAVE DEBT — **72**

PART II: HOW TO BUILD THE LIFE YOU WANT

CHAPTER 4: DREAM — 76
- Envision Your Ideal Day — 78
- Your Path, Your Rules — 79
- Discover the Deeper Motivation Behind Your Goals — 80
- What If You Still Don't Know What You Want? — 81
- Take the First Step – Even If It's Small — 83

CHAPTER 5: EARN — 98
- Build Skills That Pay (and Light You Up) — 100
- How to Start Building Skills That Pay — 101
- How to Stand Out (At Every Stage) — 102
- Spending Smart in a World That Wants You Broke — 107
- Budget For Freedom — 111

CHAPTER 6: INVEST — 118
- What the Stock Market *Really* Is (And Isn't) — 120
- Index Funds: The Smarter Way to Invest — 121
- Investment Accounts: Where Your Money Grows — 123
- Saving vs. Investing — 128
- Putting It All Together — 131
- Definitions — 132

CHAPTER 7: FREEDOM — 136
- Choose the Freedom Path That Fits You — 137
- Creating Career Freedom — 138
- Why Planning Breaks Matters, Even Now — 140
- What is Financial Freedom – Really? — 142
- Find Your FIRE — 144

CONCLUSION — 152
GLOSSARY — 154
INDEX — 162
ABOUT THE AUTHOR — 168
CONNECT — 170

Preface

PREFACE

I grew up with a mom who was smart, loving, creative, and determined, but like so many people, she didn't have the tools to manage money. I remember seeing her at the kitchen table, crying over handwritten budgets, trying to make it all work. She worked multiple jobs and started a business out of our apartment, cutting paper and gluing notepads together just to earn extra income. No one worked harder than she did.

But hard work alone isn't enough if you don't have the right information. My mom had everything she needed *except* access to the financial knowledge that could've changed everything.

Because of that, I got a front-row seat to what financial stress really looks like. We moved around a lot. Sometimes we didn't have stable housing. I remember living in our car. I remember pulling donated clothes out of black trash bags, wishing I could shop at the mall like other kids. That longing just to feel normal, to have enough, stuck with me.

My mom believed education was the key to a better life, and she pushed hard to make sure my sister and I got the best one possible. That meant I ended up in schools surrounded by middle-class and upper-class kids who had way more than we did. I started setting financial goals pretty early on: have my own money, live somewhere stable, and buy new clothes straight off the rack. My first job was at the Gap, and trust me, I made the most of that employee discount.

As a teenager, I started reading personal finance books to figure out how money worked. A lot of what I found said things like, "Debt is good," or "Use credit to support your lifestyle." So I believed that. I thought having a car note, a mortgage, and a stack of credit cards was just what people did. That being in debt was normal, and maybe even a sign that you were doing well.

It wasn't until later that I found a completely different message: that real wealth doesn't come from debt, it comes from freedom. Freedom to choose how you spend your time. Freedom to walk away from people, jobs, or systems that don't serve you. Freedom to build the life you want.

When I stopped following the advice that led me deeper into debt and started learning from people who had actually *built* wealth, everything changed. I started to feel something I hadn't felt in a long time...peace. Instead of waiting for my next paycheck to fix things, I had money saved. Instead of spending every dollar, I had options. I finally understood what financial freedom really meant.

And here's what I want you to know: **You don't have to wait until you're older to build wealth. You can start right now.**

Money isn't just about buying things. It's about freedom. It's about being able to breathe, rest, take care of yourself, and say yes to what really matters. It's about choosing your own future, not having it chosen for you.

This book is here to help you start. You're about to learn the basics of how money works, how to avoid common traps, and how to build real wealth step by step. By the end, you'll have a plan. One that's designed for your life, your goals, and your version of freedom.

With love,

Paris

Introduction

INTRODUCTION

You've been doing everything right. You're focused on school, trying to set yourself up for a good future, and probably hearing from everyone around you how important it is to "get good grades" so you can "go to college" and "get a good job." But here's the real question: will doing all that actually make you rich? Or even just comfortable?

I used to think the answer was yes. But then I started seeing people who followed all the rules and were still living paycheck to paycheck. That didn't make sense to me. If working hard and going to school was the key, why were so many adults still broke, stressed, and stuck in jobs they hated?

It turns out most of the financial advice we're given is designed to keep people right in the middle; not rich, but not poor either. Just working hard enough to survive. And when you do try to get ahead, you're told to go into debt to do it. "Use credit cards to build your credit." "Take out loans to go to school." "Buy a new car. It's normal." But all of that debt ends up holding people back, not helping them get ahead.

Here's what no one tells you: **You don't need to be rich or famous to build wealth. You just need a smart plan and the right mindset.**

That's what this book is all about. I wrote it to give you the money guide I wish someone had handed me when I was your age. Not some boring textbook. Not another lecture from an adult who doesn't understand your life. Just straight-up real talk about how money actually works, what traps to avoid, and how to create real freedom for yourself starting now.

WHY IS THIS INFO SO HARD TO FIND?

Let's be honest. The world makes a lot of money off people who are struggling. There are whole industries built around keeping folks in debt: credit cards, payday loans, buy now/pay later apps, overpriced colleges. If everyone learned how to win with money early on, a lot of these companies wouldn't make a dime. So instead of teaching us how to build wealth, we're taught how to borrow and spend. But I want more for you. I want you to have options.

Imagine what life could look like if money wasn't constantly stressing you out. If you could travel, help your family, take breaks when you need them, and say yes to opportunities that light you up instead of only the ones that pay the bills. That's what financial freedom looks like.

HOW THIS BOOK WILL HELP YOU GET THERE

This book is split into two parts:

- **Part One** helps you stay out of the debt trap, including credit cards, car loans, and student debt.
- **Part Two** helps you build the life you want using real tools and strategies that actually work. You'll learn how to earn money, spend smarter, invest early, and plan for the kind of freedom most people don't experience until retirement (if ever).

INTRODUCTION

You don't have to wait until you're older to get your money right. In fact, the earlier you start, the easier it is to get ahead.

So if you're ready to stop just surviving and start building a life you're excited about, this book is for you.

PART ONE

How to Stay Out of the Debt Trap

CHAPTER 1
Credit

CHAPTER 1 • CREDIT

My mom couldn't contain her excitement. I was headed to college as our family's first college graduate in the making. And I was going to Harvard, of all places! It felt like the final round of a championship game we'd been playing together for years, a mother-daughter dream team with perfect chemistry.

My mom had spent my whole childhood making sure I was in schools that matched my potential. She showed up to every parent-teacher conference, advocated for me when unfair rules popped up, and transferred me to better schools when the environment wasn't helping me grow. She even got me into my city's gifted program, which meant I attended the best public high school in the state. On top of that, she was my biggest cheerleader, reminding me to rest when I was stressed and nudging me forward when I doubted myself.

So here we were: Harvard, here we come.

Along with telling everyone she knew (neighbors, church members, the cashier at the grocery store…), my mom was determined to send me off with *everything* I might possibly need. We scrolled through online "College Must-Have" lists and wandered through big-box stores with shiny back-to-school displays. According to the lists, I needed it all: organizers, shower caddies, mirrors, storage bins, under-bed boxes, rugs, sheets, comforters, wall posters, lamps, an iron, a hair dryer, a new laptop, you name it.

Here's the part no one told me: college move-in season is basically the Super Bowl for credit card companies. Every store we visited was "kind enough" to offer me, an 18-year-old with *no* financial history, a shiny new credit card right at checkout. And they didn't just offer the card; they dangled a 10% or 15% discount on my purchase if I applied on the spot. To me, that felt like free money.

By the end of that summer, I had boxes and boxes of stuff, a wallet stuffed with store credit cards, and a brand-new identity: broke and in debt before my first class even started.

WHY SO MANY ADULTS STRUGGLE WITH DEBT

If you've ever heard an adult say, "I just can't seem to get ahead," there's a good chance debt has something to do with it. Debt is sneaky. It usually starts small, with a single purchase you can't pay for in full right away. But over time, it grows, adding interest charges that make the total amount owed bigger and harder to pay off.

A lot of adults fall into debt because they've been taught that it's "normal." Need a car? Finance it. Want a new phone? Put it on a payment plan. College? Take out loans. Clothes, vacations, even groceries? Swipe the card and deal with it later. The problem is "later" always comes, and it's often more expensive than you thought.

Credit cards are one of the biggest traps. They make it easy to spend money you don't actually have. If you only pay the *minimum payment* each month, it can take years (or even decades) to pay off the balance because of something called **compound interest**. That's when interest is charged not just on what you borrowed, but also on the interest you haven't paid yet. It's like a snowball rolling downhill, getting bigger and bigger.

Sometimes debt happens because of emergencies like a medical bill, a car repair, or a job loss. Without an emergency fund, people

CHAPTER 1 • CREDIT

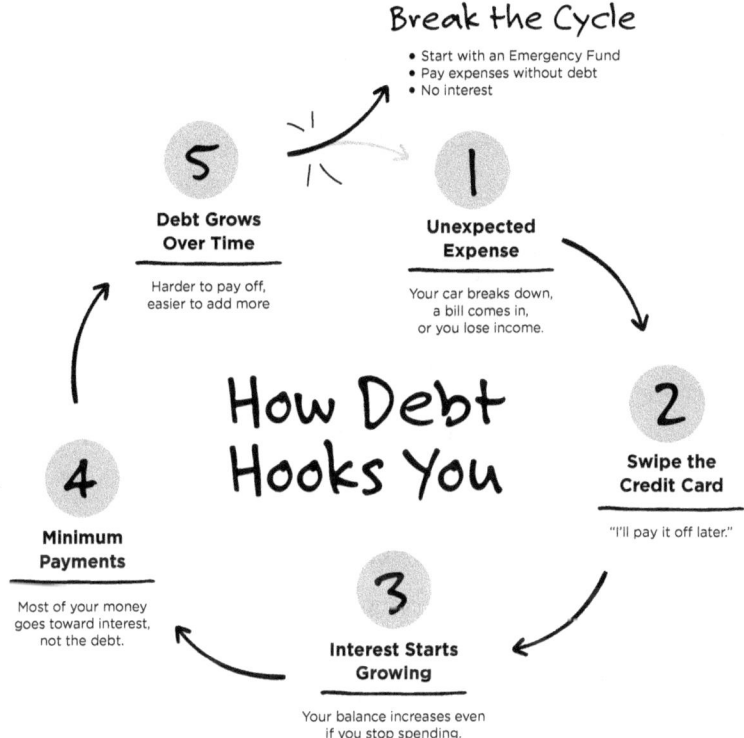

have no choice but to borrow. Other times, it's about spending more than you earn, especially when social media and advertising convince you that you "need" things you can't afford yet.

Here's the truth: most people don't set out to bury themselves in debt. It happens little by little, until the payments are eating up so much of their paycheck that it feels impossible to catch up. The good news? You can learn to see the warning signs early and avoid the debt trap before it even starts.

THE TRUTH ABOUT CREDIT

When I got my first credit card at 18, nobody sat me down to explain exactly how credit works. I just knew it was a shiny piece of plastic that let me buy things instantly, and I could pay for them "later." That word *later* is where a lot of people get into trouble.

Credit is basically a way of borrowing money from a bank, store, or lender. You agree to pay it back, usually with **interest**, a fee for using their money. If you pay the full balance by the due date, you avoid interest. But if you carry a balance, you'll start paying extra every month just for the privilege of borrowing.

Here's what most people don't realize: every time you use credit, your choices are being recorded in a **credit report**. This report shows your history of borrowing and paying back money. It's used to create your **credit score**, a three-digit number that tells lenders how risky it is to lend to you. A high score can help you get better deals on loans and even make it easier to rent an apartment. A low score can cost you thousands of dollars in higher interest rates over your lifetime.

The credit industry can feel like a game that's rigged against beginners. You need credit history to get the best interest rates, but if you mess up early, those mistakes can follow you for years. That's why it's important to understand a few basics from the start:

1. **Always pay on time.** Late payments are one of the fastest ways to tank your credit score.

2. **Keep your balance low.** Experts recommend using less than 30% of your available credit.

3. **Don't apply for too many cards at once.** Every application creates a "hard inquiry" that can lower your score temporarily.

THE MINIMUM PAYMENT TRAP

When I first started using credit cards, I thought making the "minimum payment" each month meant I was doing great. After all, the credit card company sent me a bill that said: **Minimum Payment Due: $25.**

That sounded totally doable. I figured as long as I paid that amount, I was being responsible.

What I didn't realize was that the minimum payment isn't designed to help you get out of debt. It's designed to help the credit card company make more money off you.

Here's why. When you only pay the minimum, most of your payment goes toward **interest**, which is the extra money you owe for borrowing. Very little goes toward your **principal**, the actual amount you charged. That means your balance barely moves from month to month, and the interest keeps piling on.

This is called **compound interest**. It means you are charged interest on what you borrowed and on the interest you didn't pay last month. Over time, it's like your balance is growing in the background while you're busy living your life.

Here's a real example:

- Let's say you charge **$1,000** on a card with a 20% interest rate.
- If you only pay the $25 minimum each month, it will take you **over 5 years** to pay it off and you'll pay more than **$600 in interest.**

Credit can be a *tool* or a *trap*. The choice is yours.

CHAPTER 1 • CREDIT

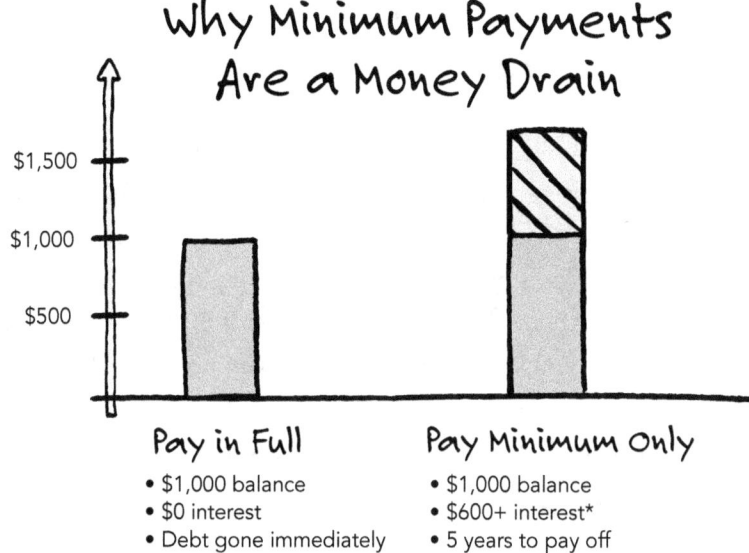

- That's more than half the original amount, just in fees.
- Credit card companies love minimum payments because they stretch out your debt for years, keeping you on the hook. The solution? Always try to pay your balance in full, or at least pay much more than the minimum. Even an extra $20 or $50 a month can shave years off your repayment time. I recommend paying your balance in full every time.

When you understand the math, you see that "minimum payment" really means "maximum profit… for them."

> Interest charges build on top of other interest charges, so the longer you take to pay, the faster your balance grows.

YOUR CREDIT SCORE: FRIEND OR FOE?

When I was in college, I thought having a credit card meant I was officially "adulting." What I didn't realize was that every swipe was affecting something I barely understood: my **credit score**.

Your credit score is basically your money report card. It's a three-digit number, usually between **300 and 850**, that tells lenders how likely you are to pay back what you borrow. The higher the number, the more "trustworthy" you look and the easier it is to get approved for loans with low interest rates.

Here's the breakdown of what makes up your score:

- **Payment history (35%)** – Do you pay your bills on time? Even one missed payment can hurt.
- **Amounts owed (30%)** – How much of your available credit are you using? This is called your **credit utilization ratio**, and experts recommend keeping it under 30%.

> *If your limit is $1,000, try to keep your balance under $300 at any time.*

- **Length of credit history (15%)** – How long have you been using credit? Longer histories look better.
- **New credit (10%)** – Opening too many new accounts at once can make you look risky.
- **Credit mix (10%)** – Lenders like to see that you can handle different types of credit. For example, a revolving account (like a credit card you pay in full each month) and an installment account (like a secured loan) show variety.

CHAPTER 1 • CREDIT

But here's the key: credit mix only makes up about 10% of your score. It's not worth taking on debt just for this factor. If you're building credit responsibly with one account, you're doing just fine.

A **credit report** is the full file behind your score. It's a record of your credit accounts, payment history, and any negative marks like late payments or collections. You're entitled to a free copy once a year from each of the three major credit bureaus (**Experian, Equifax,** and **TransUnion**) at **AnnualCreditReport.com.**

Here's the thing: credit scores can be your best friend or your worst enemy. If you pay on time and keep your balances low, your score can open doors to better housing, cheaper car insurance, and lower rates on loans. But if you ignore your bills and max out your cards, your score can drop fast and climbing back up takes time.

When you're just starting out, focus on using credit sparingly and paying every bill on time. Your future self will thank you when it's time to rent your first apartment or qualify for a mortgage.

HOW TO BUILD AN EMERGENCY FUND (EVEN ON A SMALL BUDGET)

Most people who think they're "good with credit" find out the hard way that debt is waiting for them when an emergency hits. Cars break down. Phones shatter. Teeth need root canals. Layoffs happen. It's not a matter of *if*, but *when*.

In those moments, it's tempting to reach for a credit card. That's why so many people say, "I keep this one card for emergencies." Sounds smart, right? But here's the truth: it's a trap. That "emergency" will cost way more than the actual bill once interest piles on.

Step-by-Step to Your Safety Net

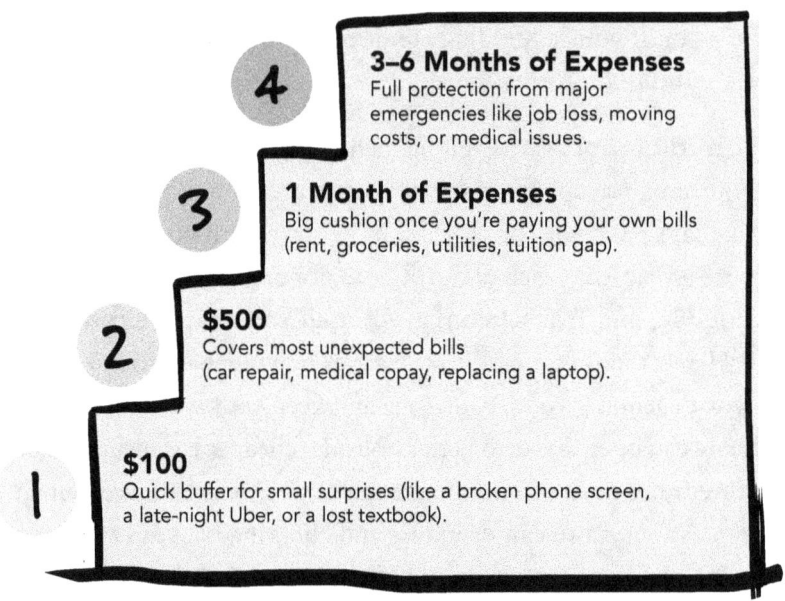

4 — **3–6 Months of Expenses**
Full protection from major emergencies like job loss, moving costs, or medical issues.

3 — **1 Month of Expenses**
Big cushion once you're paying your own bills (rent, groceries, utilities, tuition gap).

2 — **$500**
Covers most unexpected bills (car repair, medical copay, replacing a laptop).

1 — **$100**
Quick buffer for small surprises (like a broken phone screen, a late-night Uber, or a lost textbook).

The better strategy? Build your own safety net with an *emergency fund*. This is money you set aside for life's surprises so you can handle them without debt. Bonus: while it's sitting in a savings account, your money earns interest instead of costing you interest. Even if the interest is small, you're moving forward instead of backward.

And here's the real magic: having your own stash of cash makes emergencies feel smaller. A $500 car repair? Instead of panic and stress, you pay it and move on. No scrambling. No long-term payments.

Start small and build over time. Every step gives you more freedom.

If you're just getting started, now is the perfect time to practice. Open a savings account and start building your "starter" emergency fund. A few hundred dollars is a huge win at this stage. Add to it whenever you get money from a birthday, a paycheck from a part-time job, a summer gig, or even leftover scholarship or stipend money. Let it sit there untouched. Not for Robux (my nephews' weakness) or that must-have outfit (mine in high school).

As your responsibilities grow to maybe paying your own phone bill in college, covering rent with roommates, or buying groceries, your emergency fund should grow too. Eventually, aim to have 3–6 months' worth of living expenses. That's about how long it can take to find a new job if you lose yours. If you own a car, a house, or have pets, consider what big surprise expenses could come your way and build your fund until you could handle them.

An emergency fund isn't just about money, it's about peace of mind. I want you to know that no matter what happens, you'll never have to swipe a credit card just to survive. That's how you keep control of your future.

HOW TO USE CREDIT WITHOUT GETTING TRAPPED

Credit scores do matter in today's world. Insurance companies often use them to set your rates. Banks check them when you apply for a loan. Landlords look at them when deciding whether to rent to you.

Technically, you could live without a credit score. Some people do it on purpose. They avoid credit entirely and accept small inconveniences like providing a deposit for rentals. But if you want to take the more common route and build a strong score, you must approach credit like a wild animal: admire it from a safe distance and never forget it can hurt you.

Here's the golden rule: **never carry a balance. Ever.** The moment you let a balance roll from one month to the next, you've stepped onto the debt treadmill. That treadmill is designed to keep you running in place forever.

If you want to use credit for the sole purpose of building your score, keep your usage under 30% of your limit, but aim for 0%. For example, if your card has a $1,000 limit, that means spending less than $300 in a month and then paying it off in full before the due date. But honestly, I recommend spending only on things you already budget for and then paying it off right away, even before the bill comes.

Safe Credit Habits

✓ Use for ONE predictable monthly bill.

✓ Keep usage under 30% of limit.

✓ Pay in full every month.

✓ Cut up the card to avoid temptation.

Debt Traps to Avoid

✗ Carrying a balance.

✗ Using for wants instead of needs.

✗ Paying only the minimum.

✗ Using multiple cards for spending.

One way to do this without temptation: use your credit card only for a predictable monthly bill, like your cell phone, then set the bill to autopay from your bank account. Once it's set, cut up the card and throw it away. That way, you'll build credit history, your utilization stays low, and you'll never be able to swipe your way into debt.

I learned this lesson the hard way. At 18, I thought credit cards were just a convenient way to pay for things. By my 30s, my balances had exploded to $20,000. It took years of discipline to dig myself out, and I never want to go back. That's why I treat credit with extreme caution now, and why I want you to decide today how you'll handle it.

Your choice is simple:

- Avoid credit entirely and skip the risks, or
- Use it only with strict rules that keep your balance at $0.

Either way, you win because you'll never give your money to the debt machine.

> The longer you take to pay, the more you give the bank instead of keeping for yourself.

A Quick Word on Other Debt Traps

Credit cards aren't the only way companies keep people in debt. Payday loans, "buy now, pay later" programs, and store financing plans often seem like quick fixes, but they're designed to make you pay way more than the item ever cost. Payday loans have sky-high interest rates that can keep you in a constant cycle of borrowing, while "buy now, pay later" plans often lead to overspending and missed payments that damage your credit. The bottom line: if you can't pay for it in full with money you already have, it's not worth the risk.

notes

CHAPTER 1
Summary

- **Debt is a trap** – Credit card companies design their products to make you spend more and pay interest for years.
- **Emergencies are predictable** – It's not a matter of *if* but *when* something unexpected will happen.
- **Skip the "credit card for emergencies" advice** – Use an emergency fund instead so you can cover surprise expenses without debt.
- **Start small with savings** – Even $100–$300 in a separate account is a win; add to it monthly and resist dipping into it.
- **Aim for 3–6 months of expenses** – Once independent, grow your emergency fund to cover job loss or large bills.
- **Credit scores matter** – They affect car insurance rates, mortgages, and rental applications.
- **Living without credit is possible** – You can avoid credit altogether, but it requires extra paperwork and deposits.
- **If you do use credit, set guardrails** – Keep balances under 30% of your limit, pay in full monthly, and automate predictable bills only.
- **One smart hack** – Put a fixed bill (like your phone) on a credit card, then cut up the card to avoid temptation.
- **Other debt traps to avoid** – Payday loans, "buy now, pay later" plans, and store financing are just as risky as credit cards.
- **Learn from my mistake** – I racked up $20,000 in credit card debt and spent years digging my way out.
- **Your action step** – Decide now if you'll live without credit or use it with strict guardrails, and keep building your emergency fund.

CHAPTER 1
Reflection Questions

1. What messages have you received about credit from your family, school, or social media? How have these messages shaped your view of credit cards?

2. Have you ever been offered a credit card or felt pressure to get one? How did you respond, and why?

3. Can you think of a time when someone you know used credit to cover an emergency expense? What were the short- or long-term results?

4. How would having a fully funded emergency fund change the way you respond to unexpected expenses?

5. What kind of relationship do you want to have with credit in the future? What values or priorities are shaping that choice?

6. What is one step you can take this month to either build your emergency fund or set up a credit guardrail?

CHAPTER 2
Car$

CHAPTER 2 • CARS

Who doesn't love the idea of hopping into a brand-new car and driving off into the sunset? It's part of the American Dream, and in December 2006, I was ready to live it. I'd just graduated from Harvard, started my first full-time job, and was traveling the country for work. The only problem? My job was based in rural New Hampshire. After years of zipping around Boston on buses and subways, I was now stranded on campus, bumming rides off coworkers (this was pre-Uber). By Christmas break, I decided it was time for my first big purchase: a car of my own.

I did some research online on affordable sedans like Toyotas or Hondas, but once I got home to St. Louis, all that went out the window. My family had connections to Chrysler, so we headed straight there for the "discount." A friendly salesman skipped the sedans and ushered us over to the shiny new 2007 Dodge Caliber. Big tires for the snow, a drink cooler in the glove box, a flashlight in the back: features perfect for "someone my age."

One short test drive later, and I was sold. When the salesman said my credit was good enough to buy without a cosigner, my mom beamed with pride. He asked how much I wanted to pay per month. I answered, "As little as possible," and he suggested a six-year loan at $360 a month. My family reassured me, "You won't even have this car in six years, so go for it!"

I signed on the dotted line and drove away in my brand-new car, and $15,000 in debt. What I didn't realize was that I'd just locked myself into years of payments, interest, and financial stress over a car that would lose thousands in value the moment I left the lot. That single choice became one of my biggest money regrets.

WILL YOU NEED A CAR – AND HOW TO DECIDE

If you're anything like I was growing up, you've probably dreamed of the day you'd have your own set of wheels. A car can represent independence, the freedom to go wherever you want, whenever you want. But here's the thing: having a car also comes with major costs and responsibilities, and rushing into ownership without thinking it through can trap you in unnecessary expenses for years.

Before deciding whether you *need* a car, ask yourself some key questions. How do you currently get around to school, work, sports practice or your friends' houses? Could you keep using those same options for a while longer? Public transportation, biking, carpooling, or even a combination of these might work just fine, especially if your school, job, or activities are nearby. If you're in college or heading there soon, you might find that having a car is more of a hassle than a help. Some campuses charge high parking fees, limit where you can drive, or make it unnecessary because everything is within walking distance.

Also think about timing. If you're not yet working enough hours to cover your own gas, insurance, and maintenance, a car might actually limit your freedom instead of increasing it because your money will be tied up in keeping it running.

Here's the truth: plenty of people wait until after school, if ever, to buy a car. They save a ton of money in the process and avoid debt that comes from rushing into a purchase too soon. If you can hold off until you really *need* a car, you'll be in a much better position to buy one you can truly afford, and enjoy, without it becoming a financial burden.

THE REAL COST OF A CAR (AND HOW TO AVOID GETTING TRAPPED)

Did I convince you to at least *think about* a car-free life? Okay, maybe you're like most Americans and believe owning a car is a necessity (I'm not judging you, I own one too). For most people, it's not owning the car that gets them into trouble; it's **how** they pay for it.

Financing, aka taking out a loan to buy a car, is the most common way people get cars these days. You walk into a dealership, sign a stack of papers, and drive away in a shiny new ride with a monthly payment hanging over your head like a ball and chain for the next several years. Sounds a little too easy, right? Ever wonder why?

Let's break it down. The typical new car loses over half its value in the first five years (about 55% on average[1]). That means if you buy a $10,000 car, you've basically tossed $5,500 out the window just by owning it for a few years. Financing a car that's dropping in value so quickly means you're likely "underwater" on your loan almost immediately, meaning you owe more than the car is worth. If you wanted to sell it, you wouldn't be able to get enough to pay off your loan. You're stuck.

To see how this plays out in real life, check out the chart on the next page. Notice how the car's value drops sharply while the loan balance barely moves. This is the trap so many buyers fall into.

---

1 Chris Hardesty, "How to Beat Car Depreciation" "Kelley Blue Book" (website), July 24, 2025, https://www.kbb.com/car-advice/how-to-beat-car-depreciation

Car Depreciation vs. Loan Balance

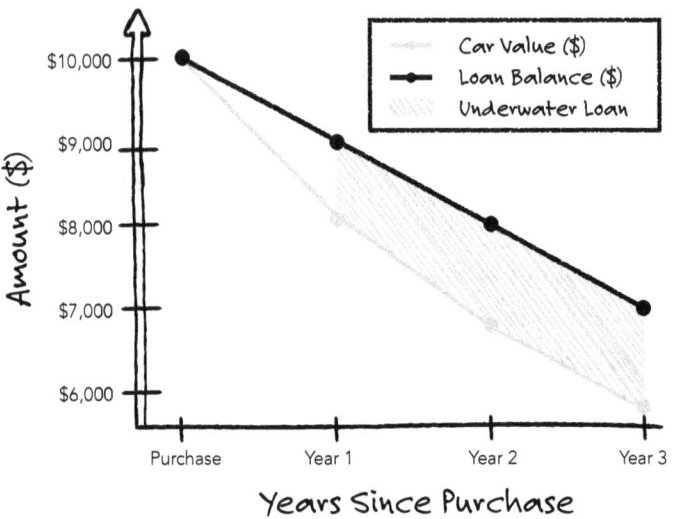

Why You're Underwater Before You Even Get Home:
See that steep drop? That's your car's value tanking the second you leave the lot. Meanwhile, your loan balance is crawling down at a snail's pace. This is how people get stuck paying for a car they can't even sell for enough to cover what they owe.

A car payment can cost you your future freedom.

Then there's the actual cost. According to Experian's 2025 State of the Automotive Finance Market Report, the average monthly loan payment for a new car today is over $700. That's before adding insurance, which is most expensive for newer cars. I remember one of my students, a freshman in college, whose parents encouraged her to buy a brand-new car. She was paying over $800 a month for it while going to school full-time and working a minimum-wage job. Even as an adult with a career, I told her I couldn't imagine taking on a payment that big.

Car payments eat up a huge chunk of your monthly budget. Once you add gas, parking, and maintenance, it's easy to see why so many people feel broke even when they're working hard. Here's what the real monthly costs can look like and how much you could free up by going for a cheaper car or even a car-free lifestyle.

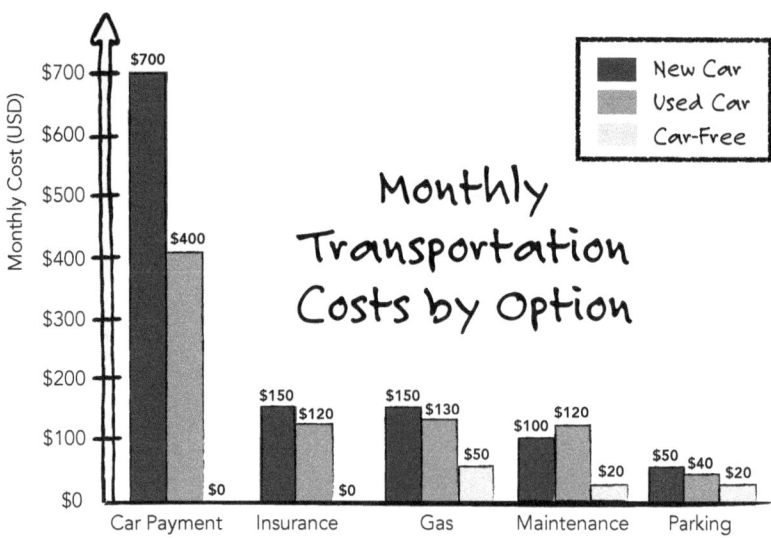

CHAPTER 2 • CARS

> **That Car Payment Is Costing You More Than You Think.** Add it up: loan, insurance, gas, maintenance, parking, and suddenly your car is eating a huge slice of your monthly pie. That's money you could be putting toward freedom instead of funneling into a hunk of metal that's losing value every day.

A massive car payment can hold you back from saving for emergencies, building wealth, or having the freedom to take advantage of opportunities. If you already have one of these loans, think about how you can get out of it as quickly as possible. And if you don't? Let's keep it that way.

HOW TO OWN A CAR WITHOUT GOING BROKE

If you decide that owning a car is the right choice for you, there's a smart way to do it; one that doesn't drain your bank account for years. The two golden rules are simple:

1. **Buy used.**
2. **Pay cash.**

Break these rules, and you risk tying up huge chunks of your income in payments, interest, and insurance. All for an asset that's losing value every day.

WHY "USED" DOESN'T MEAN "JUNK"

When some people hear "used car," they picture a clunker with missing hubcaps and a high likelihood of breaking down on the way home. But the reality is different. Many used cars are only a few years old, in great condition, and still under warranty.

Why? Because millions of Americans lease cars and turn them in after two or three years. Those vehicles often show up on the lot as **certified pre-owned**, which means they've passed inspections, are backed by the manufacturer, and often come with a warranty.

You can also find deals from rental car companies (like Enterprise) that sell their cars after a few years, often including extended warranties.

Tools to Try

- **Kelley Blue Book** (kbb.com) – Check fair market value before buying.
- **Carfax** (carfax.com) – See the vehicle's history, including accidents.
- **Enterprise Car Sales & Carvana** – Options for no-haggle pricing.

Dealership vs. Private Seller

- **Dealerships**: Easier process, warranty options, less risk; but prices are higher because of dealer markups.
- **Private Sellers**: Lower prices, but more risk. Always check the KBB value, run a Carfax report, and get the car inspected by a mechanic before you commit.

> ### Smart Used Car Buying Checklist
> 1. Set your budget.
> 2. Look up fair market value on Kelley Blue Book.
> 3. Check the vehicle's history on Carfax.
> 4. Get a pre-purchase inspection from a trusted mechanic.
> 5. Negotiate or buy at a fair price (no-haggle options are available).

IF YOU CAN'T PAY CASH YET

Here's some tough love: if you can't pay cash for a car, you can't afford a car without stress.

Financing, especially with "no money down" offers, often keeps people in debt for years. High interest rates and immediate depreciation mean you'll be "underwater" (owe more than it's worth) from day one.

Instead:

- Buy the cheapest reliable car you can afford now, even if it's not your dream ride.
- Work extra hours, start a side gig, or sell unused items to boost your savings.
- Trade up gradually as you save more cash.

It's the **slow-cooker method** instead of the **microwave method**, but you'll own your car outright and keep your freedom.

MY CAR STORY

That brand-new car I bought years ago? It cost me an extra **$5,000 in interest** on top of the purchase price, plus higher insurance, maintenance, and parking costs.

Even worse, I still owed more on it than it was worth when I started my debt-free journey. I couldn't just sell it and walk away.

I started making extra payments and paid it off months ahead of schedule. Suddenly, I had hundreds of extra dollars each month. I drove that car for 13 years, saving thousands. When it finally died in 2019, I sold it to CarMax for $1,000 and bought my next lightly used car in cash.

> **Bottom Line:** Don't let your car own you. By buying used, paying cash, and avoiding debt, you can save thousands, free up money for your goals, and still drive something reliable.

notes

CHAPTER 2
Summary

- **Two golden rules for smart car ownership** – Buy used and pay cash.

- **Why buying new is a money trap** – Cars lose value fastest in the first 3 years, making new cars a poor investment for financial freedom.

- **Buying used doesn't mean buying junk** – Many used cars are 2–3 years old, well-maintained, and still under warranty.

- **Key tools for smart buying** – Use Kelley Blue Book for pricing, Carfax for history, and no-haggle sites like Enterprise Car Sales or Carvana.

- **Dealership vs. private seller** – Dealerships offer convenience and warranties but cost more; private sellers can be cheaper but riskier.

- **If you can't pay cash, you can't afford it** – Avoid financing, especially "no money down" offers that keep you in debt.

- **Start with the cheapest reliable car** – Save consistently and trade up over time.

- **The "slow-cooker method"** – Work extra, take on side gigs, or sell items to build cash and upgrade gradually.

- **My car story** – A new car led to $5,000 in interest; paying it off early and driving it for 13 years saved thousands.

- **Financial freedom impact** – Avoiding a car payment can free up $400–$800/month for investing, travel, or big goals.

CHAPTER 2
Reflection Questions

1. Think about your current (or future) transportation needs. Could you realistically get around without owning a car? Why or why not?

2. If you do own a car, what emotions come up when you think about its costs: pride, stress, frustration, freedom? Why do you think you feel that way?

3. What's the earliest memory you have of wanting a car? How do you think advertising, peer influence, or culture shaped that desire?

4. Imagine your life without a monthly car payment. What would you do with the extra money each month?

5. Have you ever been tempted to buy "more car" than you could afford? What might have motivated that decision: status, convenience, habit, or something else?

6. What is one practical step you could take in the next year to either avoid a car loan or pay off an existing one faster?

CHAPTER 3
Education

CHAPTER 3 • EDUCATION

So far, we've talked about two of the most common sources of debt: credit cards and car loans. I hope you've taken a moment to reexamine your beliefs and habits in these areas and maybe even decided to make some big changes in how you use credit or how you approach buying a car. At the very least, I hope you've created a plan to reduce any debt you have, or to keep avoiding it if you've made it this far without borrowing a dime.

Now let's turn to one of the most important topics for anyone who wants more options in life: **postsecondary education** (education after high school). I'm not just talking about traditional four-year universities. When I say "postsecondary education," I mean any training or learning you pursue beyond a high school diploma, whether that's a bachelor's degree, an associate degree, trade or technical school, an industry-recognized credential, or a certificate program that gives you the skills to land a good job.

The research is clear: most good-paying careers today require some form of postsecondary credential.[1] The challenge is that the cost of these programs, especially traditional college, has skyrocketed. Over the past few decades, as federal and state governments pulled back funding, schools shifted the costs onto students through higher tuition and fees. At the same time, more people than ever began enrolling in postsecondary programs, which drove demand and prices even higher. Add in predatory lending practices, and it's no wonder we now have a full-blown student debt crisis.

For too many people, the path to a degree or credential is paved with student loans they'll be paying back for decades. In fact, student loan debt is now the second-largest type of consumer debt in

---

[1] Anthony P. Carnevale, et. al., "After Everything: Projections of Jobs, Education, and Training Requirements through 2031," Georgetown University Center on Education and the Workforce, 2023.

WHAT COUNTS AS POST

(When we say "college," we

4-Year College or University

Earn a **bachelor's degree** in a field of study. Often the path for careers that require advanced knowledge, research, or professional licensing (e.g., engineering, accounting, teaching).

2-Year Community College

Earn an **associate degree** or prepare to transfer to a 4-year program. Also offers lower-cost training in high-demand careers like nursing, IT, and law enforcement.

Trade or Technical School

Get hands-on training for specialized careers like welding, cosmetology, or automotive repair in **months, not years**.

SECONDARY EDUCATION?

mean ALL of these options.)

Apprenticeships

Earn a wage while learning a trade from experienced professionals. Combine **on-the-job training** with classroom instruction, often leading to industry-recognized credentials.

Industry Certifications

Prove your skills in a specific field, such as IT, healthcare, or project management, through recognized exams and courses. Can often be completed in weeks or months.

Online Credentials

Flexible, self-paced learning from accredited institutions or recognized platforms. Includes certificates, micro-credentials, and bootcamps in fields like coding, business, or design.

> **Bottom Line:** A "postsecondary credential" is <u>any</u> recognized qualification you earn after high school that opens doors to better jobs and higher pay, whether it's in a classroom, on a job site, or online.

the United States, second only to mortgages.[2] And unlike a house or a car, you can't sell your education to pay off what you owe. It's with you for life. Federal loans can be hard enough to pay off, but private loans often come with higher interest rates, fewer protections, and less flexibility if you run into financial trouble.

That doesn't mean you should give up on getting an education after high school. It does mean you have to be strategic. The goal is to get the credential you need for the career you want while taking on as little debt as possible, or, ideally, no debt at all. I've spent years helping students do exactly that, using a mix of smart school selection, scholarship strategy, and careful planning to graduate without student loans. In this chapter, I'm going to show you how to do the same, whether you're pursuing a degree, a trade, or any other training program that will set you up for success.

WHY STUDENT LOANS CAN BE RISKY

With all the headlines about student loan forgiveness and the high cost of education, you might wonder if postsecondary training is worth pursuing at all. The short answer: absolutely.

Research shows that adults with a degree or industry-recognized credential earn more over their lifetimes and are less likely to face long-term unemployment than those without one.[3] These benefits are especially visible during economic downturns. In the early months of the global pandemic, many service and low-wage jobs vanished overnight as restaurants, hospitality, and retail shut

---

[2] Hanson, Melanie. "Student Loan Debt vs Other Debts" EducationData.org, February 25, 2025, https://educationdata.org/student-loan-debt-vs-other-debts

[3] U.S. Bureau of Labor Statistics, "Education Pays, 2024" (website), May 2024, http://bls.gov/careeroutlook/2025/data-on-display/education-pays.htm

down. Meanwhile, plumbers, electricians, and other skilled trades stayed in demand, and many office workers kept their jobs by shifting to remote work.

Why Postsecondary Education Still Matters

- **Higher Lifetime Earnings** – Adults with a degree or industry-recognized credential earn significantly more over their lifetimes than those without one.
- **Stronger Job Stability** – Credential holders are less likely to face long-term unemployment, especially during economic downturns.
- **Career Flexibility** – A credential opens doors to a wider range of jobs, even outside your original field of study.
- **Competitive Advantage** – In today's job market, many middle-class careers require *some* form of postsecondary education just to get in the door.

That doesn't mean all credentials are created equal, or that earning one guarantees a six-figure salary. But, when chosen wisely, a postsecondary credential acts like career insurance. Even if you don't end up working in your original field, the credential itself often opens doors to better-paying, more secure, and more fulfilling opportunities.

Given these benefits, it's no wonder so many people assume student loans are a good investment. But here's the problem: life is unpredictable. People change majors, shift career paths, or

Getting into school debt is easy but getting out isn't.

sometimes leave school altogether. And while your career may change, your debt will not. The psychological weight of student loans follows you regardless of your salary, and for those who don't graduate, it's an even heavier burden.

Student loans drain your paycheck month after month, just like credit cards or car loans, but with even more traps built in. Federal loans offer multiple payment plans and forbearance options, which can stretch repayment over decades while you keep paying interest. And unlike most debt, student loans are very hard to discharge in bankruptcy.

The Student Loan Trap

- Not easily erased through bankruptcy.
- Interest accrues during deferment/forbearance.
- Flexible repayment plans can keep you in debt for decades.

Trust me and the millions of Americans still making payments years after graduation. Borrowing for school can limit your financial freedom for decades. In the rest of this chapter, I'll show you how to get the education you need without taking on student loans at all.

STEP 1: FIND THE TRUE COST OF SCHOOL

Despite what you might hear in our debt-burdened society, it is entirely possible to earn a postsecondary credential without going into debt. The key is knowing (1) the real cost of your school and (2) how you'll cover it.

Colleges have a "sticker price" (published tuition and fees) and a "net price" (what you'd actually pay after financial aid). Every college is required to have a Net Price Calculator on its website, usually under "Financial Aid." Search the school name + "net price calculator" to get an estimate based on your academic and financial profile.

EXAMPLE 1: COLLEGE A

One college lists tuition, fees, room, and board at **$50,000 per year**. That's the sticker price. When you enter your family's income, your GPA, and other details into the school's Net Price Calculator, it might show:

- Sticker Price: $50,000
- Estimated Grants & Scholarships: −$35,000
- Estimated Work-Study: −$2,000
- **Estimated Net Price (after aid): $13,000**

Important: Work-study isn't money the school subtracts from your bill upfront. It's money you can *earn* during the school year through a part-time job, which you can then use to cover part of your costs.

EXAMPLE 2: COLLEGE B

Now compare that to another college with a much lower sticker price: **$25,000 per year**. The calculator might show:

- Sticker Price: $25,000
- Estimated Grants & Scholarships: −$5,000
- Estimated Work-Study: −$2,000
- **Estimated Net Price (after aid): $18,000**

Takeaway: Even though the second college looks cheaper at first glance, the *net price* ends up being higher than the first college because the aid package is smaller. That's why using each school's calculator matters. You want to know the *true* cost before making decisions.

STEP 2: MATCH YOURSELF TO FUNDING SOURCES

Here's where your background and strengths can guide your search:

STUDENT BACKGROUND	FUNDING SOURCES
Talented	Merit scholarships
Low-income	Need-based scholarships
Low-income + high-achieving	Colleges that meet 100% of demonstrated need
Middle-income, middle-achieving	Outside scholarships + cash flow

STUDENTS WITH ACADEMIC, ATHLETIC, OR MUSICAL TALENT

If you're a strong student, athlete, or musician, merit-based scholarships should be your first target. These awards are typically based on grades, test scores, or demonstrated talent.

Academic scholarships often come directly from colleges or from national organizations such as the National Merit Scholarship Corporation (based on PSAT scores). Other well-known programs include the Jackie Robinson Foundation, the United Negro College Fund, Coca-Cola Scholars, and the Gates Foundation.

Athletic and music scholarships are also plentiful. Coaches, band directors, or program leaders may have connections to recruiters. If not, check college websites for requirements and reach out directly to coaches or music program directors; especially at smaller schools that actively seek out talent.

STUDENTS FROM LOW-INCOME FAMILIES

Need-based scholarships are awarded based on your family's financial situation. The most common source is the federal government, accessed through the **Free Application for Federal Student Aid (FAFSA)** at FAFSA.gov. Submit the FAFSA starting in October for the following school year to see if you qualify for the **Pell Grant** (over $7,000 per year as of this writing) and other federal, state, and institutional grants.

> As of 2026, the maximum Pell Grant is over $7,000/year, but check current figures at studentaid.gov for the latest amount.

Your chosen school's net price calculator will estimate this aid so you can plan for what's left to cover.

HIGH-ACHIEVING STUDENTS FROM LOW-INCOME FAMILIES

Top-performing students from low-income households can access some of the most generous aid packages in the country. Many elite colleges promise to meet **100% of demonstrated financial need**, which can mean a full ride.

To find these schools, search for "colleges that meet 100% of demonstrated need." In addition, apply to programs like the Ron

Brown Scholar Program, the Jack Kent Cooke Foundation, and QuestBridge, which provide both funding and long-term advising.

STUDENTS WHO DON'T FIT A CATEGORY

If none of the above apply, focus on **shopping for the best value**. Public colleges in your state offer **in-state tuition**, which is heavily subsidized for residents.

If a four-year program is still too expensive, consider starting at a community college. Complete your first two years at a lower cost, earn an associate degree, and transfer to a four-year school to finish your bachelor's.

Also look for **local and regional scholarships** as these often have fewer applicants. Check with your high school counselor, community organizations, and the financial aid pages of the schools you're considering.

STEP 3: FILL THE GAP WITHOUT LOANS

Once you've identified your most affordable option, create a **budget and payment plan.**

- Save from part-time jobs while still in high school (aim for at least $500 to cover books and initial expenses).
- Explore payment plans through your school.
- Consider employers or programs that cover tuition such as **AmeriCorps**, Starbucks (partnership with Arizona State University), or military service benefits.

> **Bottom Line:** There are many pathways to an affordable or even free credential. The goal is to graduate with skills and opportunities, not a lifetime of student loan payments.

DEBT-FREE COLLEGE PLAYBOOK

STEP 1

Find the True Cost

- Go to your school's website → Financial Aid section → Net Price Calculator
- Or, search: "[School Name] net price calculator"
- Write down your **Net Price** (what you'll really pay after aid).

STEP 2

Match Yourself to Funding Sources

YOUR BACKGROUND	MAIN TARGETS
High grades / athletic / music talent	Merit scholarships (college + national orgs like National Merit, Jackie Robinson, Coca-Cola)
Low-income	FAFSA → Pell Grant + state + school need-based grants
Low-income + high-achieving	Colleges meeting 100% of need + QuestBridge, Jack Kent Cooke, Ron Brown
Middle-income / middle-achieving	Public in-state schools, community college, local/regional scholarships

Your Step-By-Step Guide to Earning Your Degree Without Student Loans

STEP 3

Reduce Costs Before You Start

- **In-state tuition for residents**
- **Start at community college** → transfer
- Compare **total degree cost** across schools before committing

STEP 4

Fill the Gap Without Loans

- Save from part-time work before/during school (aim: $500+ before start)
- Tuition payment plans (spread costs across months)
- Employer & program benefits: AmeriCorps, Starbucks, Military GI Bill
- Apply for local scholarships (less competition)

STEP 5

Commit to Your Plan

- Set a semester-by-semester budget
- Re-apply for aid & scholarships each year
- Keep grades up to maintain merit awards
- Graduate on time to avoid extra costs

Goal: Graduate with a degree or credential and a clear path forward, without a single student loan payment holding you back.

MAKE GOOD CHOICES

In this chapter, we've focused heavily on the cost of education, but cost isn't the only factor to consider. Your educational choices should ultimately be based on what you want to do with your life, not money alone. These decisions are some of the most important you'll ever make, shaping the opportunities available to you for years to come.

Too often, smart and capable students give up on the idea of college or advanced training because they assume they can't afford it. That's a mistake. Many of our families haven't navigated the higher education process before. Only about one in three adults in the U.S. have a bachelor's degree or higher.[4] This means the people giving you advice may mean well, but still be misinformed. Even those who went to college years ago may not know about the wide range of options available today.

Sometimes, well-meaning adults give advice that misses the mark. When I was in high school, one of my teachers suggested I join the military instead of going straight to college because she knew my family didn't have much money. Even Michelle Obama's high school counselor told her she "wasn't Princeton material." She went on to graduate from Princeton and earn her law degree from Harvard, proving that the people who doubt you can be wrong.

The truth is that the job market has changed. Our economy has shifted from factory-based to service-based, and now we're in a knowledge-based economy. Most well-paying jobs today require education or training beyond high school. That's why it's so important to do what you can to get educated. Once you have your credential, follow the career strategies I share later in this book to make sure your education translates into a well-paying job and a meaningful career.

---

[4] Melanie Hanson, "Education Attainment Statistics" EducationData.org, January 14, 2025, https://educationdata.org/education-attainment-statistics

Don't Let Money Make the Decision for You

Plenty of smart students walk away from college or training programs because they think they can't afford it. That's not you. There are scholarships, grants, work programs, and other funding options out there, even if your family has never been through this process before.

Remember:
- People who doubt you can be wrong (just ask Michelle Obama).
- There are more ways to pay for school than you think.
- The right education can open doors for the rest of your life.

Don't let someone else's limited perspective limit your future.

WHAT I WISH I KNEW EARLIER

I was lucky to attend Harvard College on a full, need-based scholarship because my family earned so little. Even though I graduated with some debt, none of it was from student loans. Just those credit cards I'd opened (another mistake we've already talked about).

But my student-loan-free streak didn't last. A year later, I went back to Harvard for a master's degree. Instead of looking for scholarships or working to help cover costs, I took out loans for the entire cost of attendance, nearly $60,000. Big mistake. If I'd waited until I was working at Harvard, I would have gotten a big tuition discount as an employee. But I didn't think about ROI (return on investment) back then. I just thought, "This is what you do, you get more degrees."

Paying those loans off took nearly 12 years. I tried repayment plans that lowered my monthly bill but barely touched the balance. I even took breaks (forbearances) when money felt tight. The problem? Interest kept piling on. Years later, I still owed almost as much as I'd borrowed. Eventually, I refinanced into a low-interest private loan through SoFi so I couldn't use flexible payment plans as an excuse to delay. I started making big extra payments whenever I could. In January 2020, I made my final payment. It felt like the weight of a car was lifted off my chest, and I swore I'd never take on another student loan again.

When I decided to earn my doctorate, I did things differently. I chose a top-ranked public university, paid in cash, and kept working full-time. I already earned a six-figure salary doing work I loved. The doctorate was a want, not a need, so I chose a program that aligned with my interests, my career, and my financial goals without taking on debt.

> **Bottom Line:** Getting into debt for school is easy. Getting out can take years. The good news? There are ways to earn a degree or credential for little or no cost, whether it's at your local public university, a community college, a trade program, or even a private school with generous aid. Don't let anyone convince you loans are the only way forward.

notes

CHAPTER 3
Summary

- **Postsecondary means more than college** – Community colleges, trade schools, apprenticeships, industry certifications, and online credentials all count.

- **Credentials boost your future** – They increase lifetime earnings, reduce unemployment risk, and expand career options.

- **Debt can erase the benefits** – The student loan system keeps many borrowers paying for decades with interest-heavy repayment plans.

- **Avoid loans if possible** – Choose affordable programs, seek scholarships and grants, and work while studying to limit costs.

- **Choose with purpose** – Base your education decisions on your goals and interests, not just cost. And plan carefully.

- **Learn from my journey** – I graduated undergrad debt-free but took on costly graduate loans that took over a decade to repay.

- **Low-cost, high-quality options exist** – Motivated students can find affordable or free programs with research and persistence.

CHAPTER 3
Reflection Questions

1. What have you been taught by family, school, or society about the value of a college degree? Do you agree or disagree, and why?

2. How do you feel about taking on student loan debt? Do you see it as a necessity, a risk, or something to avoid at all costs?

3. If you imagine your ideal postsecondary path, what would it look like? (Include your field of study, location, and lifestyle while in school.)

4. What scholarships, grants, or tuition-free options are you already aware of? Where could you look to discover more?

5. If you had to completely fund your education without loans, what creative strategies could you use to make it work?

6. How could starting your career without student loan payments change your life and financial freedom timeline?

IF YOU ALREADY HAVE DEBT

You've just read about the biggest money traps that can hold students back: credit cards, cars, and student loans. The goal is to help you avoid these traps in the first place. But maybe as you're reading, you're thinking:

Too late. I've already signed for student loans. Or I've got a car note. Or I've swiped a credit card I couldn't pay off.

If that's you, listen closely: **you are not doomed.** Debt does not define you. What matters is the choices you make starting today.

The good news? You can still build the life you want. Here's how to take control and move toward freedom:

1. STOP DIGGING THE HOLE

The first step is to press pause on any new debt. That means:

- Don't swipe a credit card unless you can pay it in full.
- Don't finance a new car while you're still paying for the old one.
- Think very carefully before taking out more student loans, especially private ones.

Every new debt makes it harder to move forward. Say no now so you can say yes to bigger opportunities later.

2. KNOW WHAT YOU OWE

Write it down. Every balance, every interest rate, every minimum payment. Don't guess. Facing the numbers might feel scary, but it's powerful. You can't change what you won't confront.

3. SORT THE URGENT FROM THE MANAGEABLE

- **High-interest debt** (like credit cards or personal loans) is urgent. Focus on these first because they drain your money the fastest.
- **Lower-interest debt** (like federal student loans in deferment or a car loan with a decent rate) can wait. Pay the minimums and keep moving.

4. ATTACK HIGH-INTEREST DEBT FIRST

Make at least the minimum payment on everything, but throw any extra money you can find at the debt with the highest interest rate. That's the one costing you the most. Knocking it out frees up cash and energy for everything else.

5. SHIFT BACK TO FREEDOM-BUILDING

Once the high-interest stuff is under control, return to the wealth plan laid out in this book:

- Build a starter emergency fund.
- Invest early. Even small amounts count.
- Keep your focus on building wealth, not just paying bills.

A FINAL WORD ON DEBT

Debt can feel like the *sunken place*, that trapped state where you can't move forward and someone else is calling the shots. But you don't have to stay there. Every payment, every decision not to borrow, and every step you take toward freedom is proof that you're moving in the right direction.

Debt doesn't define you. Your choices from this moment forward do.

PART TWO

How to Build the Life You Want

CHAPTER 4

Dream

CHAPTER 4 • DREAM

"What would you do if you knew you couldn't fail?"

I kept that quote on my wall growing up. It's a powerful question. If success were guaranteed, what would you try? What dream would you pursue?

Asking myself that question has led me down an incredible path: traveling the country to connect students with life-changing opportunities, driving policy changes to make college more accessible, founding a nonprofit in my community, visiting nearly every continent, living in different cities, recording a studio album, and earning my doctorate.

But one day, in a program for early-stage philanthropists in education, I was asked a different version of the question: *"What would your life look like 20 years from now?"* This wasn't about my next step, it was about my long-term vision. And that's harder than it sounds. We change over time. The career, city, or lifestyle you dream about at 15 or 20 might not fit you at 35 or 40.

I think about a friend who spent decades working toward her childhood dream of becoming a lawyer, only to find she hated it once she got there. Her story, and research from psychologists[1], confirms something important: we're actually pretty bad at predicting what will make us happy in the future. That's why this chapter isn't about creating the *perfect* life plan you have to stick to no matter what.

Instead, it's about learning to walk toward the future you want, starting with what excites you right now, and being open to evolving along the way. Because life happens in the *journey*, not just at the destination.

Dreaming about your future isn't just an exercise in imagination. It's about identifying the feelings, experiences, and freedoms you want most, then finding ways to bring them into your life

---

1 Daniel Gilbert, *Stumbling on Happiness*, Vintage, 2007.

now. The truth is, most of us don't just want money for its own sake. We want the *freedom* we think it buys: freedom from money stress, freedom to design our own days, freedom to do work that matters, and freedom to share our gifts with the world.

When I did the 20-year vision exercise, mine was clear: financial freedom for myself and for the next generation. I pictured coaching leaders, serving on advisory boards, flying to New York to see Blue Ivy Carter perform on Broadway, and smiling at the knowledge that I had bought my freedom. No longer working because I had to, but because I wanted to. I imagined a world where my community, my family, and I were all free to live on our own terms.

ENVISION YOUR IDEAL DAY

Now that you've heard my dream, let's get crystal clear on yours. Asking, *"What would you do if you knew you couldn't fail?"* can push you to imagine a life that inspires and excites you.

Give yourself the time and space to go deep. Find a comfortable spot, maybe put on some music that makes you feel good, close your eyes, and start picturing your ideal life. Then use the "My Ideal Day" section (pp. 86–87) or grab a notebook or journal to capture what you see.

Think through the details:

- What does a typical day look like from the moment you wake up to the moment you go to bed?
- What kind of work do you do? What projects light you up? Who are you working with?
- Are you traveling? Where to, and what are you doing there?

- How are you spending time with family or friends? What does it feel like?
- What hobbies, activities, or experiences fill your free time?

Here's the key: don't worry about *how* any of it will happen. This isn't about being realistic or building a plan. It's about dreaming big. Let yourself write down anything that excites you, no matter how wild it sounds. You'll know you've landed on something real when just thinking about it makes you feel lighter, happier, or more energized.

Once you've written it all down, capture every detail that matters to you. There's nothing too big or too small to include.

Do you feel good about what you've written? Good. Now, rest your pen for a moment while I tell you a story.

YOUR PATH, YOUR RULES

A smart businesswoman once visited a small coastal village and met a local woman who made her living fishing. Curious, the businesswoman asked how her days went.

"Every morning," the fisher said, "I take my boat out, drop my nets where I know the fish will be, and after a few hours, I have enough for the day. I sell my catch at the market, then spend the afternoon relaxing with friends and family. At night, I enjoy a good meal and a glass of wine on the beach with my partner while we watch the sunset."

The businesswoman leaned in. "You're incredibly skilled. If you bought a bigger boat and hired some help, you could catch more fish and make more money. Eventually, you could sell to other cities. Maybe even the whole country."

The fisher nodded slowly. "And if I did all that, what would I do with the extra money?"

"Well," the businesswoman said, "you could keep expanding, buy more boats, hire more people, and eventually have a multimillion-dollar business."

"And then?"

"Then you could retire rich and spend your days however you wanted."

The fisher smiled. "But… that's exactly what I do now."

DISCOVER THE DEEPER MOTIVATION BEHIND YOUR GOALS

When you hear the parable of the businesswoman and the fisher, you might think its message is that a leisurely life where work plays a smaller role and leisure takes precedence is more valuable than building a large, successful business. That's a perfectly valid interpretation, and likely the one the original storyteller intended.

But I want to challenge you to look from a wider vantage point. There's room in the world for both the businesswomen and the fishers. The real question is: which set of activities would bring *you* joy?

What if the businesswoman genuinely loved building businesses? What if she found deep satisfaction in spotting opportunities, creating systems, and refining them until they ran beautifully? She might spend her ideal life doing exactly that. Not because she "had to," but because it lit her up. Meanwhile, someone like the fisher might value a life with a different rhythm, balancing work and leisure, and prioritizing time with friends, family, and personal passions.

CHAPTER 4 • DREAM

The deeper lesson is this: your dream life is less about the *what* and more about the *why*. Pick one important element of your vision. Maybe it's a certain career, travel goal, lifestyle, or hobby. Ask yourself why it matters. Then, keep going. Just like the fisher asking the businesswoman a series of "And then what?" questions, you can keep asking yourself "Why?" until you've peeled back the layers. Use pages 88–89 to help you think this through.

Try going at least five "whys" deep. You may find that what you want isn't just about the surface-level goal, but it's about a core value, feeling, or experience at the root. Freedom. Connection. Mastery. Creativity. Peace.

Once you know your *why*, you can make better decisions about *how* to get there and you'll have a vision that truly belongs to you.

WHAT IF YOU STILL DON'T KNOW WHAT YOU WANT?

If you've been struggling to picture your dream life, you're not alone. It's actually *really* hard to imagine things we've never experienced. On top of that, research shows we're not always great at predicting what will make us happy in the future.

The good news? You don't have to have it all figured out right now. You can discover what you like, and what you don't, by paying attention to your daily life.

STEP 1 – NOTICE WHAT YOU ENJOY

Over the next week or two, use pages 90–91 or the notes app on your phone to write down:

- **Things that make you happy** – moments when you smile, feel energized, or get excited.
- **Things you don't enjoy** – moments that leave you feeling bored, stressed, or frustrated.

Examples:

- *Liked* – Helping a friend edit their TikTok video, leading your soccer warm-up, solving a tricky math problem.
- *Disliked* – Waking up super early for activities, long unstructured group projects, sitting through events with no breaks.

STEP 2 – LOOK FOR PATTERNS

After a week or two, read over your notes.

- Circle your **Top 5 Joys** – things that show up often and matter most to you.
- Circle your **Top 5 "No Thanks"** – things you'd love to avoid in your future.

STEP 3 – IMAGINE MORE OF THE GOOD STUFF

Ask yourself:

- If I had way more of my favorite things in my life, what would that look like?
- If I could avoid my "No Thanks" list completely, how would my days feel?

STEP 4 – DRAFT YOUR FIRST VISION

Write a short paragraph about your future based on what you discovered. It doesn't have to be perfect, it just has to feel exciting and true for who you are *right now*.

> **Quick Tip:** Your vision will change as you grow and experience new things. That's normal. Just keep paying attention to what lights you up and what drags you down. Every time you update your list, you're getting closer to the life you actually want.

TAKE THE FIRST STEP – EVEN IF IT'S SMALL

You've started building a vision for your future. Now it's time to stop just *thinking* about it and start *trying it out*.

Don't worry, you don't need a ton of money or years of planning to begin. The rest of this book will walk you through the steps to financial freedom, but you can start living little pieces of your dream *today*.

MINI-EXPERIMENTS FOR YOUR FUTURE LIFE

Pick one part of your vision and find a way to test it out now. Make notes on pages 92–93 if you'd like.

If you want to travel…

- Search for the city online. Look at photos of landmarks, read about local foods, and watch videos from people who live there.
- Use Google Maps "Street View" to virtually walk the streets.
- Try cooking a recipe from that place or check out a book or movie set there.

If you want to live near water...

- Spend the day at a nearby lake, river, or beach. Bring snacks, music, and a notebook to jot down how it feels to be there.
- Volunteer with a local nature group that works on the water.

If you want to be a leader...

- Run for a leadership role in a school club.
- Volunteer to organize a group project or help plan an event.

If you want to be a creator...

- Want to write a book? Start by jotting down your ideas or writing one scene.
- Want to perform? Sign up for a school talent show or a local open mic night.

WHY START SMALL?

When you try things now, you:

- Learn whether you actually like them.
- Gain skills and confidence for the future.
- Keep your motivation high because you're already living parts of your dream.

> **Your Challenge:** Before you turn the page, take <u>one small action</u> toward your dream life. It could be as quick as researching something for 10 minutes or as big as signing up for a new opportunity. Once you've had even a little taste of your future, you'll be hooked. And you'll be ready for the next step: figuring out how to pay for it.

Start living pieces of your dream life *right now.*

my ideal day...
SEE PAGES 78–79 FOR INSTRUCTIONS.

SEE PAGES 80–81 FOR INSTRUCTIONS.

SEE PAGES 81–83 FOR INSTRUCTIONS.

STEP 1 – WHAT DO YOU ENJOY?

STEP 2 - WHAT PATTERNS DO YOU SEE?

STEPS 3 AND 4 - IMAGINE MORE OF THE GOOD STUFF AND DRAFT YOUR VISION

mini-experiments

SEE PAGES 83–84 FOR INSTRUCTIONS.

notes

CHAPTER 4
Summary

- **Your dream life is unique to you** – Don't copy someone else's path. Focus on what you actually want.

- **Figure out your "why"** – Ask yourself "Why?" about your goals until you get to the real reason they matter to you.

- **If you're not sure what you want yet...** – Pay attention to your daily life. Write down what you enjoy and what you don't. Patterns will appear over time.

- **Start now, even in a small way** – Test-drive your dreams through small actions you can take today.

- **The more you try, the clearer your vision becomes** – Real-life experiences help you refine what you want and give you confidence to go after it.

CHAPTER 4
Reflection Questions

1. If success were guaranteed, what is one dream you would pursue and why does it excite you?

2. When you picture your ideal day 20 years from now, what are the details that stand out most clearly? What do those details say about what matters to you?

3. Think about the fisher and the businesswoman story: which lifestyle feels closer to your dream life right now, and why?

4. Pick one goal or dream you've thought about. Ask yourself "Why does this matter to me?" five times in a row. What deeper value or feeling do you discover at the core?

5. Looking back at the last week, what were 2–3 moments that made you feel energized or happy? How might those moments shape your vision for the future?

6. What is one small experiment you could try this month to test out a piece of your dream life? Something quick, fun, or low-risk that could give you a taste of what you want?

CHAPTER 5
Earn

CHAPTER 5 • EARN

Ever since I was a little girl, I dreamed of traveling the world. I'm not sure when it started…maybe when I realized I was named after a famous city. But I do remember the first time I had the chance to leave the country.

I was in eighth grade and had just started at a new school after testing into the gifted program. One of the most exciting parts of my new school was that I got to choose a foreign language for the first time. I picked Spanish because I thought it would be the most useful. Everything was going smoothly, until one day, the French teacher announced that her class would be going on a trip to Paris, France.

Paris! My name is Paris! I knew I had to find a way to go on that trip. The only problem? I wasn't in the French class. Still, I worked up the courage to ask the French teacher, who didn't even know me, if I could join. To my surprise, she said yes. All I needed was to come up with a couple thousand dollars to pay for it.

That's when reality hit. My family didn't have extra money lying around. Most months, it was a stretch just to cover the basics. But my mom had always told us, *"You have not, because you ask not."* She encouraged us to speak up about what we wanted, even if it seemed impossible. I think she could see how badly I wanted this, because she immediately got to work. She organized a fundraising raffle in my name, asking local friends to donate goods and services as prizes. My whole family pitched in to sell tickets at church, at sporting events, anywhere we could.

Before I knew it, the trip was paid for, and I was booked on my first-ever international flight. That trip taught me something I've never forgotten: where there's a will, there's a way.

In the last chapter, you dreamed about what you want your future to look like. Now it's time to take the next step: figuring out how to earn the money to make it happen.

BUILD SKILLS THAT PAY (AND LIGHT YOU UP)

When it comes to building wealth, there's a simple three-step formula:

1. **Earn more money**
2. **Spend less than you earn**
3. **Invest the rest**

Most people focus on cutting back on spending, but a faster path to financial freedom is learning how to **earn more, even while you're in school.**

You've probably heard the advice: *"Follow your passion."* Here's the truth: passion matters, but it's not enough on its own. Passion gives you energy and motivation, but it's the **skills you practice and master** that make you valuable and allow you to get paid well. As author Cal Newport argues, people who become "so good they can't be ignored" usually get there through deep practice, not by chasing vague passions.[1]

I think the two ideas actually work together. Passion gives you the drive to practice longer, harder, and better. Practice builds the skills that employers, clients, or customers will pay for. Together, passion and practice unlock opportunity.

---

1 Cal Newport, *So Good They Can't Ignore You: Why Skills Trump Passion in the Quest for Work You Love*, Grand Central Publishing, 2012.

CHAPTER 5 • EARN

Ever since I was a little girl, I dreamed of traveling the world. I'm not sure when it started...maybe when I realized I was named after a famous city. But I do remember the first time I had the chance to leave the country.

I was in eighth grade and had just started at a new school after testing into the gifted program. One of the most exciting parts of my new school was that I got to choose a foreign language for the first time. I picked Spanish because I thought it would be the most useful. Everything was going smoothly, until one day, the French teacher announced that her class would be going on a trip to Paris, France.

Paris! My name is Paris! I knew I had to find a way to go on that trip. The only problem? I wasn't in the French class. Still, I worked up the courage to ask the French teacher, who didn't even know me, if I could join. To my surprise, she said yes. All I needed was to come up with a couple thousand dollars to pay for it.

That's when reality hit. My family didn't have extra money lying around. Most months, it was a stretch just to cover the basics. But my mom had always told us, *"You have not, because you ask not."* She encouraged us to speak up about what we wanted, even if it seemed impossible. I think she could see how badly I wanted this, because she immediately got to work. She organized a fundraising raffle in my name, asking local friends to donate goods and services as prizes. My whole family pitched in to sell tickets at church, at sporting events, anywhere we could.

Before I knew it, the trip was paid for, and I was booked on my first-ever international flight. That trip taught me something I've never forgotten: where there's a will, there's a way.

In the last chapter, you dreamed about what you want your future to look like. Now it's time to take the next step: figuring out how to earn the money to make it happen.

BUILD SKILLS THAT PAY (AND LIGHT YOU UP)

When it comes to building wealth, there's a simple three-step formula:

1. Earn more money
2. Spend less than you earn
3. Invest the rest

Most people focus on cutting back on spending, but a faster path to financial freedom is learning how to **earn more, even while you're in school.**

You've probably heard the advice: *"Follow your passion."* Here's the truth: passion matters, but it's not enough on its own. Passion gives you energy and motivation, but it's the **skills you practice and master** that make you valuable and allow you to get paid well. As author Cal Newport argues, people who become "so good they can't be ignored" usually get there through deep practice, not by chasing vague passions.[1]

I think the two ideas actually work together. Passion gives you the drive to practice longer, harder, and better. Practice builds the skills that employers, clients, or customers will pay for. Together, passion and practice unlock opportunity.

---

1 Cal Newport, *So Good They Can't Ignore You: Why Skills Trump Passion in the Quest for Work You Love*, Grand Central Publishing, 2012.

When I started working in education, I earned much less than my friends in other fields. For years, I assumed that was just the way it was. But then I met people in the *same field* making double what I made. That's when I realized I had been selling myself short.

I started asking questions: What jobs paid more? What skills did I need? How could I prepare for those interviews? Within months after researching higher-paying roles, networking, and getting help with my résumé, I landed a job that paid more than twice my old salary. It made me wish I had started asking those questions much earlier.

The lesson? **You don't have to choose between doing something you love and earning a good salary. You can, and should, aim for both.**

HOW TO START BUILDING SKILLS THAT PAY

STEP 1: EXPLORE & RESEARCH

- Find out what people earn in the jobs you're curious about. Use sites like Glassdoor.com or Indeed.com to check salary ranges.
- Ask people in those roles. Instead of "What do you make?" try: "What's the typical salary range for your position?"

STEP 2: BUILD SKILLS NOW

- Increase your skills and experience where you are. If you want to work in tech, try a coding course. If you're interested in healthcare, shadow someone at a hospital.

- Say yes to opportunities that both **pay and teach**, like a part-time job, tutoring, or a freelance gig that gives you marketable skills.

STEP 3: GAIN PROFESSIONAL EXPERIENCE

- Apply for internships, research assistant positions, or campus jobs tied to your field of interest. Even short-term gigs can lead to bigger opportunities.
- Keep leveling up. Use online courses, side projects, or networking to open doors to higher-paying roles.

Passion isn't a magic ticket, but it is powerful fuel. Use what excites you to drive the kind of deep practice that builds skills. Then, use those skills to open doors to higher-paying opportunities. The sooner you start building both passion *and* practice, the sooner you'll be ready for work you love and work that pays.

HOW TO STAND OUT (AT EVERY STAGE)

Whether you're applying for a summer job, an internship, a leadership role, or your first full-time position after graduation, the rules for standing out are surprisingly similar. The earlier you start building these skills, the more natural and powerful they'll become.

1. NETWORK BEFORE YOU APPLY

Most people think of "networking" as something adults do at conferences, but it's just a fancy word for building relationships. People like to hire or recommend people they already know.

Student Steps to Earning More

You don't have to wait until after graduation to start boosting your income. Start where you are and build from there:

Step 1: EARLY JOBS
(HIGH SCHOOL / FIRST WORK EXPERIENCE)

✓ Babysitting, tutoring younger students, pet sitting, lawn care, retail, or food service.

✓ Sell something you make or collect like art, crafts, clothing, baked goods, sneakers, or thrifted finds.

Step 2: SIDE HUSTLES & FREELANCE WORK
(HIGH SCHOOL + COLLEGE)

✓ Offer services you're good at like photography, graphic design, music lessons, or social media help.

✓ Enter competitions or apply for scholarships that award cash or prizes for skills you already have.

Step 3: PROFESSIONAL EXPERIENCE
(COLLEGE / EARLY CAREER)

✓ Apply for paid internships in fields you're curious about.

✓ Take online courses (many are free) to learn high-demand skills like coding, video editing, or digital marketing. Then use them for freelance or campus jobs.

✓ Ask questions and network: talk to adults in careers you admire to learn what they did and how much they earn.

- **In high school:** Ask teachers, coaches, counselors, family friends, and even older students if they know someone in the field or organization you're interested in. A science teacher might know someone at the local hospital, or a coach might know someone hiring for a part-time job.
- **In college:** Tap into your professors, career center, alumni network, or student organizations. Many internships and job opportunities are passed along informally within these circles.
- **In adulthood:** Networking often makes the difference between sending a résumé into a black hole and getting a warm introduction to the hiring manager. It's how many high-paying jobs are landed before they're even posted.

2. TREAT EVERY CONVERSATION LIKE AN INTERVIEW

When you talk to people about opportunities, remember: they're sizing you up. Even an informal coffee chat is a chance to show you're prepared, respectful, and serious about your goals.

- **In high school:** This might be a conversation with your debate coach about a recommendation letter or a friend's parent about a part-time job.
- **In college:** A chat with a professor during office hours or with a visiting speaker at a campus event can open doors to internships and research roles.
- **In adulthood:** The same principle applies when you're meeting potential employers, collaborators, or mentors. A strong first impression often leads to introductions that can change your career.

3. PERFECT YOUR MARKETING MATERIALS

Think of your résumé, cover letter, and online profiles as your personal billboards. They should communicate your value at a glance.

- **In high school:** Keep your résumé to one page. Include part-time jobs, volunteer roles, leadership positions, and awards. Use strong action verbs ("organized," "led," "created") and numbers when possible ("raised $500," "served 50 customers per shift").
  - **Example:** *Instead of "Worked as cashier at grocery store," write "Handled cash and credit transactions for 100+ customers per shift with accuracy and speed."*
- **In college:** Add internships, campus leadership, research projects, and relevant coursework. Tailor your résumé to highlight transferable skills, not just duties.
  - **Pro Tip:** *Start a LinkedIn profile if you haven't already. Think of it as your digital résumé and networking tool.*
- **In adulthood:** Highlight achievements, not just responsibilities. Use keywords from the job description and customize your cover letter for each role, showing exactly how your skills match the position.

> **Quick Resources:** Try Canva.com for free résumé templates, Novoresume.com for guided building, or your school's career center for résumé reviews.

4. BUILD YOUR ONLINE PRESENCE

Employers (and even scholarship committees or admissions officers) will look you up online. Make sure what they find reflects your goals.

- **In high school:** Google yourself and see what comes up. If there's anything you wouldn't want an employer or scholarship committee to see, clean it up. Even if you don't need LinkedIn yet, make sure your social media reflects the image you want others to see. You can also start a simple LinkedIn profile with a professional photo and short summary if you're ready.
- **In college:** Keep your LinkedIn updated, join groups related to your field, and post about projects or experiences that show your growth. A simple personal website can showcase your résumé, portfolio, or creative work.
- **In adulthood:** Consistently engage with professional content, share insights, and publish posts that highlight your expertise.

5. DON'T LEAVE MONEY ON THE TABLE

Whether it's a raise, a scholarship, or a higher starting salary, you can often get more than the initial offer if you ask.

- **In high school:** Apply for multiple scholarships, especially "stackable" ones you can combine. If you get an unpaid internship offer, politely ask if a paid option exists.
- **In college:** Some campus jobs and internships have flexible pay scales. Research the ranges, then practice asking for the higher end. Scholarships, fellowships, and grants can also help cover expenses if you know how to seek them out.

> **In adulthood:** Research salary ranges for your role (Glassdoor.com is a great resource), document your achievements, and make a clear case for why you deserve more. Even small raises compound over time.

> **Bottom Line:** The earlier you learn to network, present yourself professionally, and advocate for your worth, the easier and more profitable these skills will be at every stage. High school and college are the perfect training grounds because they give you room to practice before the stakes feel sky-high. Every opportunity you take on now builds the reputation and track record you'll carry into your career.

SPENDING SMART IN A WORLD THAT WANTS YOU BROKE

Money is easy to spend, and there are entire industries built to make sure you part with yours fast. The key to financial freedom isn't just making more money; it's keeping more of it. That means knowing what's essential, cutting the rest, and finding savings where most people never think to look.

STEP 1: IDENTIFY THE BIG STUFF

Most people try to save money by cutting small things, like skipping lattes. That's fine, but the biggest savings come from tackling your biggest expenses: **housing** (rent, mortgage, utilities), **transportation** (car payments, insurance, gas), **food** (groceries, eating out), and **technology** (cell phone, cable/streaming).

- **In high school:** You might not be paying rent yet, but you probably have tech, food, and transportation costs you can control. Learning to spot your big expenses early will make you a savings pro when you're on your own.
- **In college:** For the first time, you may be paying rent, splitting utilities, or managing a meal plan vs. groceries. These categories will be your biggest opportunities to save each semester.
- **After graduation:** Once you're paying all your own bills, these big categories will determine whether you keep hundreds or thousands of extra dollars each year.

STEP 2: SCORE QUICK WINS

Some savings are so easy, you can knock them out in an afternoon.

- **Car Insurance:** If you drive, compare rates every 6–12 months. A higher deductible usually means a lower monthly payment, and you can save the difference.
- **Cell Phone Plans:** Discount carriers often run on the same networks as big-name companies for a fraction of the price. Even $20/month plans exist if you're flexible.
- **Streaming Instead of Cable:** Cable can cost $100+ per month. Rotating streaming services based on what you actually watch can save hundreds per year.
- **High schoolers:** Even if you're not the bill-payer yet, you can help your family find these savings and show you're financially savvy.
- **College students:** You may be the one setting up your own phone or streaming plans for the first time. Start with the lowest-cost option and only add on what you truly need.

STEP 3: GET CREATIVE WITH HOUSING

Housing is usually the biggest expense, and it's the hardest one to change. But it's also where the most savings are possible.

- **Beginner moves:** Turn off unused lights, unplug electronics, and adjust your thermostat to save on utilities. Share housing with roommates instead of going solo.
- **College moves:** Consider being a resident advisor (RA) for free or discounted housing, or look into off-campus housing with roommates to reduce costs.
- **Advanced moves:**
  - **House Hacking:** *Rent out spare rooms to cover your housing costs.*
  - **Slow Flips:** *Buy a home, fix it up, live in it, and sell it for a profit.*
  - **Geo-Arbitrage:** *Move to a lower-cost city, or even another country, while earning the same income.*

STEP 4: BE REALISTIC

Saving is important, but don't make yourself miserable. Pick the changes you can stick with and let them add up over time.

> **Big Takeaway:** The earlier you learn to control your big expenses, the more financial freedom you'll have, whether that means extra money for college textbooks, travel with friends, investing in your future, or eventually buying your dream home.

CHAPTER 5 • EARN

BUDGET FOR FREEDOM

If you want all your hard work earning and saving to actually pay off, you need a plan to keep that money from quietly slipping away. That plan is called a budget. A budget is simply a system for deciding where your money will go *before* you spend it. Or put another way: **a budget is a roadmap for your money. You choose the destination before the cash leaves your pocket.** Without one, money tends to disappear without you even realizing it.

No matter your situation, whether you're getting an allowance, earning money from babysitting or a part-time job, working a campus job or internship, or later collecting a full-time paycheck, budgeting is how you make sure your money works for you instead of vanishing.

In college, you may already be handling bigger expenses like rent, groceries, or utilities. In that case, your budget isn't just a planning tool, it's a survival tool.

STEP 1: KNOW WHERE YOUR MONEY GOES

The first step is to figure out exactly where your money is going right now.

- **In high school:** Look at your allowance, job income, or any money gifts you get. If you already have bills (phone, car insurance, subscription services), list each one with its due date. If not, track categories like food, clothing, entertainment, or "just because" spending.
- **In college:** Add in financial aid refunds, work-study or part-time job income, and regular bills like rent, utilities,

groceries, or your meal plan. These can be bigger and more complex than high school expenses, but tracking them now prevents surprises.

You can do this on paper, in a spreadsheet, in the notes app on your phone, or with a free budgeting app like Goodbudget. If you have a bank account, scroll through your debit card history to see where most of your money goes.

Don't skip this step. It's like finding the holes in a leaky bucket before you try to fill it.

STEP 2: GIVE YOUR MONEY A JOB

Once you know where your money's going, it's time to make a plan for where you want it to go.

- ▸ Set spending limits for each category (food, fun, clothing, savings, giving, etc.).
- ▸ Decide how much you want to save first, then work backward to decide how much you can spend in each area.
- ▸ Write down specific goals. In high school, that might be saving for prom, a new phone, or your first car. In college, it could be textbooks, spring break travel, a study-abroad program, rent, or building an emergency cushion.

> **Pro Tip:** This is called "paying yourself first." Treat saving like a bill you owe to you. If you get in the habit now, you'll never be one of those people who says, "I'll save whatever's left at the end of the month" (spoiler: nothing will be left).

STEP 3: PICK A TRACKING METHOD

There's no single "right" way to budget. Pick one that feels doable for you:

- **The Notes App Method** – Write down everything you spend and subtract from your category totals. Simple, free, and always in your pocket.
- **Spreadsheets** – Great if you like organizing and customizing your own system.
- **Budgeting Apps** – Tools like YNAB ("You Need A Budget") or Goodbudget let you set limits, track automatically, and see where you're overspending.
- **Envelope or Jar System** – Put your money for each category into separate envelopes (or jars). When the envelope is empty, you're done. (College students sometimes use two debit cards for the same idea: one for essentials, one for "fun money.")
- **Separate Bank Accounts** – Use one account for bills, one for spending, and one for savings. If you're under 18, you can often set up multiple "buckets" inside a youth account.

STEP 4: KEEP IT FLEXIBLE BUT CONSISTENT

Your budget is a plan, not a prison. If you want to spend more in one category, you can; but only if you take that money from another category. The total you spend each month (or each paycheck) should stay the same.

As you move into adulthood, this flexibility becomes even more important. Your expenses will get bigger and more complex (rent, insurance, groceries, utilities) and the habit of adjusting without overspending will be a lifesaver.

STEP 5: AUTOMATE WHAT YOU CAN

If you're getting a regular paycheck, whether from babysitting, a part-time job, work-study, or your first full-time role, set up automatic transfers so money moves to savings the moment you're paid.

In adulthood, this will be crucial for building an emergency fund, investing for retirement, and reaching big goals like buying a home. For now, even setting aside $5–$20 from each paycheck or allowance can build the habit. Over time, you'll increase the amount.

STEP 6: CELEBRATE MILESTONES

Budgeting is not just about saying "no" to spending, it's about saying "yes" to your future. Whether you save your first $100, pay for textbooks without stress, pay off a credit card in adulthood, or hit your goal for a new car, take time to celebrate. This keeps your motivation up and makes the process fun.

> **Remember:** Budgeting now means you'll never have to say, "I don't know where my money went." The skills you build today (like tracking, planning, and adjusting) are the same ones that will help you handle a much bigger paycheck tomorrow.

Together with the first two steps of **earning more** and **spending less**, budgeting is what creates the money you'll later invest. It's one of the most important steps toward building wealth.

Next, we'll move into the final step: how to **"invest the rest"** and grow the money you've worked so hard to keep.

notes

CHAPTER 5
Summary

- **Wealth starts with three steps** – earn more, spend less than you earn, and invest the rest.

- **Earning more comes from skills plus passion** – passion fuels your drive, but it's deep practice that builds valuable skills and higher pay.

- **Standing out matters at every stage** – networking, making strong first impressions, polishing your résumé, building an online presence, and advocating for your worth open doors to bigger opportunities.

- **Big expenses matter more than small cuts** – housing, transportation, food, and tech usually make or break your budget.

- **A budget is your plan for your money** – track income and expenses, give each dollar a job, and choose a system that works for you (apps, spreadsheets, envelopes, or multiple accounts).

- **Automating savings builds wealth faster** – pay yourself first and celebrate milestones along the way to stay motivated.

CHAPTER 5
Reflection Questions

1. What are you naturally good at or passionate about that could turn into income?

2. Have you ever made money on your own through a side hustle, gig, or creative idea? How did it feel?

3. What income goals do you want to set for yourself this year? Why does that number matter to you?

4. What's one way you could stand out through networking, improving your résumé, or building your online presence that could open more opportunities?

5. When you think about your biggest expenses (like food, transportation, or tech), where do you see opportunities to save?

6. How do you currently track your money? Do you know where it goes each month? If not, what's one step you could take to start?

CHAPTER 6
Invest

CHAPTER 6 • INVEST

I first learned about something called the **FIRE movement** (**F**inancial **I**ndependence, **R**etire **E**arly) when I was deep in paying off my own debt and looking for ways to save money faster. That's how I stumbled onto the Mr. Money Mustache blog, written by Pete Adeney. Pete is what some might call an extreme saver. He doesn't own a car; he bikes or takes public transportation everywhere. He shops at low-cost grocery stores, cooks at home, cut cable, keeps his utility bills super low, and finds free entertainment instead of expensive outings.

Here's the wild part: he did all of this while married and raising a child. His family's total yearly budget? **Less than $25,000.**

At first, I thought: *Why would anyone live this way on purpose?* Pete would say it's about being economical, helping the environment, and avoiding consumer culture. But it turns out he had a bigger goal: retiring from work in his 30s.

Pete was an engineer making a solid income, though not quite six figures. Instead of spending most of it, he saved and invested the majority. He learned that a few smart investing moves could get him to financial freedom much faster than most people ever dream possible. His plan worked. He retired at 30 and hasn't worked a traditional job since.

Here's what stuck with me: Pete didn't rely on some get-rich-quick scheme. He didn't flip real estate, start a flashy business, or gamble in the stock market. Instead, he used a **simple investment strategy** that just about anyone can follow.

Since then, I've learned that thousands of other people have done something similar. There are blogs, books, Reddit threads, and even a movie (*Playing with FIRE*) all about this movement. For some, the appeal is never having to work again. For others, it's just having the **freedom** to work if they want to, travel more, or spend more time with family.

The financial advice at the heart of the FIRE approach is summed up perfectly in JL Collins's book *The Simple Path to Wealth*. He originally wrote it as a letter to his daughter, explaining how she could invest her money to have financial freedom too. His advice is simple: **invest in low-cost index funds, keep it simple, and let time do the work.**

I'm going to share that same strategy with you in this chapter. Whether you want to retire at 30 like Pete, or just want to make sure your future self never has to worry about money, learning this now gives you a huge advantage.

WHAT THE STOCK MARKET *REALLY* IS (AND ISN'T)

If you're going to learn how to invest, it's worth taking a step back to understand what the stock market actually is.

The U.S. runs on a **capitalist economy**. This means most businesses are owned by private people (not the government) and exist to make a profit for their owners. Here's the cool part: if you invest in the stock market, you can be one of those owners.

Companies sell tiny slices of ownership called **stocks** (or shares). When a company makes more money over time, the value of its stock usually goes up. If you own that stock, you share in those profits. Of course, the opposite can happen too. If the company loses money, the value of your shares can go down.

That's why some people think the stock market is like gambling. You can't know for sure which companies will do well. Even billionaires like Warren Buffett don't recommend guessing and betting on single companies. Instead, they recommend a smarter, lower-risk approach: **index funds**.

> "By periodically investing in an index fund, the know-nothing investor can actually out-perform most investment professionals."
> **Warren Buffett**

INDEX FUNDS: THE SMARTER WAY TO INVEST

An **index** is just a group of companies measured together to see how they're doing. For example:

- **S&P 500** – the 500 largest U.S. companies
- **Dow Jones** – 30 big, well-known companies
- **NASDAQ** – mostly tech companies

An **index fund** is an investment that buys stock in all the companies in a given index, automatically. That means:

- You're investing in many companies at once, so your risk is lower.
- There's no expensive manager constantly buying and selling (so fees are low).
- Your investment simply follows the market over time.

This approach has a strong track record: over the past 100 years, the stock market has gone up by about 10% a year on average. But that number doesn't tell the whole story. Prices of things like food, clothes, and housing also rise over time, which is called **inflation**. Once you factor in inflation, the "real" growth of the market is closer to 7% a year. Even if you look at any 30-year period, the market still averages around 7% growth after accounting for inflation. (This is why I use a 7% calculation for the examples in this book, which is the most conservative approach).

One of the best-known index funds is **Vanguard's Total Stock Market Index Fund** (VTSAX), which invests in the entire U.S. stock market. There's a $3,000 minimum to get started, but its cousin, **VTI**, has no minimum.

WHY THIS WORKS

Investing in index funds doesn't mean your account will only go up. Stock prices bounce around daily. But if you keep investing consistently and don't pull your money out during dips, history shows you'll come out ahead in the long run. Those "down" times? They're actually buying opportunities; shares are on sale.

Over decades, your investments will grow. Some investments also pay **dividends**, which are cash payments from the companies you own. Together, that growth can support your lifestyle later and help you build wealth to pass on to future generations.

THE BIG PICTURE

Index funds are one of the easiest and smartest ways for most people to invest. You can open an account at Vanguard.com (or a similar platform) in just minutes and start building wealth today. Unfortunately, many households in the U.S. own no stock at all, often because the stock market feels intimidating or confusing.

Learning this now gives you an advantage. You can change the story for yourself, your friends, and your family. Share what you learn with siblings, parents, or even grandparents. The earlier you start, the more powerful your money becomes. Investing early is like adding rocket fuel to your money. The longer it burns, the farther and faster it can take you.

INVESTMENT ACCOUNTS: WHERE YOUR MONEY GROWS

A generation ago, many workers didn't have to think much about retirement. Their employers gave them a pension that paid them every month for life after they stopped working. Those days are mostly gone. Now, most people have to save for retirement themselves. The good news? The tools we have today are powerful, and if you start early, your money can grow into something amazing.

Think of investment accounts as special containers for your money. You put money in, invest it (like in the index funds we just talked about), and watch it grow over time. Some of these accounts even come with tax benefits, meaning the government gives you a break on taxes to encourage you to save.

STEP 1 (DO THIS NOW IF YOU CAN): OPEN A ROTH IRA

A Roth IRA (Individual Retirement Account) is the MVP for young investors. Here's why:

- **If you're in high school:** You can open "a custodial Roth IRA" with a parent's help as long as you have earned income (from a job, side hustle, etc.).

INDEX FUNDS IN PLAIN ENGLISH

1. What's an Index?

Think of an **index** as a scoreboard that tracks how a group of companies is doing.

EXAMPLE – THE S&P 500
- 500 of the biggest U.S. companies
- Includes brands you already know: Apple, Nike, Disney
- When these companies make money, the index score goes up.

2. What's an Index Fund?

An **index fund** is like buying a little piece of *all* the companies in an index at once. Instead of betting on just one winner, you own **hundreds**.

WHY IT'S SMART:
- **Less risky** – If one company has a bad day, you've still got 499 others.
- **Low cost** – No pricey managers making guesses.
- **Proven track record** – Over decades, the market has grown 7–10% a year on average.

Share the Knowledge!
Most young people have never been taught this.
Talk to friends, tell your siblings, and show your parents!

3. From First Job to First Million

Let's say you work part-time in high school or college and invest **$25/month** in an index fund:

YEARS INVESTED	MONTHLY CONTRIBUTION	VALUE AT 7% AVERAGE GROWTH
10 years	$25	$4,300
20 years	$25	$12,700
40 years	$25	$61,800

If you keep **increasing** what you invest as your income grows, you could become a millionaire before you retire. Even if you never win the lottery.

4. How to Start (Even Before 18)

1. Ask a parent/guardian to help you open a **custodial account**, a type of account an adult manages for you until you turn 18 or 21 depending on your state (Fidelity, Schwab, and Vanguard all offer them).
2. Once your account is open, you can buy index funds. Important: Fund names often look different depending on where you invest. For example:
   - **VTI** – Vanguard Total Stock Market ETF
   - **SWTSX** – Schwab Total Stock Market Index Fund
   - **FXAIX** – Fidelity 500 Index Fund (tracks the S&P 500)
3. Set up automatic monthly contributions from your paycheck. Even $25/month adds up over time.

The earlier you start, the less you have to invest to build serious wealth.

- **If you're in college or older:** You can open your own Roth IRA directly with a brokerage like Vanguard, Fidelity, or Schwab. No parent needed.
- You use after-tax money, meaning you've already paid taxes on it, so it grows tax-free for decades.
- When you retire (after age 59½), you won't pay a penny in taxes on the money you take out; not even on the thousands (or millions) it's earned along the way.
- **Flexibility:** You can withdraw the money you put in (your contributions) anytime, without penalty. This makes it useful even before retirement, like for buying your first home.

> **Pro Tip:** Even $500 invested now can grow to over $10,000 by the time you're 60 without you adding another cent. That's the magic of starting early. Whether you're a teen with a summer job or a college student with a part-time paycheck, the earlier you start, the more time your money has to grow.

STEP 2 (DO THIS LATER WHEN YOU HAVE A FULL-TIME JOB): USE YOUR EMPLOYER'S PLAN

When you get your first full-time job, your employer may offer a retirement plan:

- **401(k)** if you work for a for-profit company
- **403(b)** if you work for a school, nonprofit, or government organization

Here's how these work:

- Money comes straight out of your paycheck before you even see it.

CHAPTER 6 • INVEST

- Your employer might **match** some of your contributions. That's free money. Always grab the match.
- Many plans offer a "target date fund" or an index fund option, which means you can invest without constant decision-making.

> **Rule of Thumb:** When you start working, contribute at least enough to get the full employer match. That's step one toward building your wealth as an adult.

STEP 3 (ADVANCED MOVE FOR LATER): REGULAR BROKERAGE ACCOUNT

Once you've maxed out your Roth IRA and 401(k)/403(b), you can invest even more through a regular brokerage account.

- No tax breaks here, but no limits either.
- You can invest for big goals before retirement, like starting a business or buying property.

THE LIFETIME INVESTING ORDER

Here's a simple checklist for your future self and your *right now* self:

1. **If you're under 18 with earned income:** Open a **custodial Roth IRA** (with a parent's help) and put in what you can.
2. **Once you have a job with benefits:** Contribute to your employer's retirement plan at least up to the company match (it's free money).
3. **Next step:** Max out your own **Roth IRA** each year, if you're eligible.

4. **Still have more to invest?** Add extra to your 401(k) or 403(b) until you hit the annual limit.
5. **Beyond that:** Invest additional money in a regular brokerage account for full flexibility.

WHY THIS MATTERS FOR YOU RIGHT NOW

Even though some of these accounts are "later" tools, understanding them now means you'll hit adulthood already knowing how to grab free money from employer matches, how to avoid tax traps, and how to grow your wealth for decades. Most adults don't figure this out until their 30s or 40s, so you'll have a huge head start.

SAVING VS. INVESTING

So far, we've focused on saving by building an emergency fund and paying off debt. Those are your first priorities.

If your job offers a retirement match, grab it (because free money is free money). Beyond that, focus on finishing these first steps before diving fully into investing. Here's why:

1. DEBT IS LIKE INVESTING... BACKWARDS

When you have debt, interest is quietly draining your money every single day. Think of it as a bucket with holes in the bottom. You can't fill it up until you plug the leaks. Paying off high-interest debt is the fastest way to start building wealth.

2. LIQUIDITY = HOW FAST YOU CAN GET YOUR MONEY

"Liquidity" is just a fancy way of saying how quickly you can turn something into cash.

Investing is how small amounts today become freedom tomorrow.

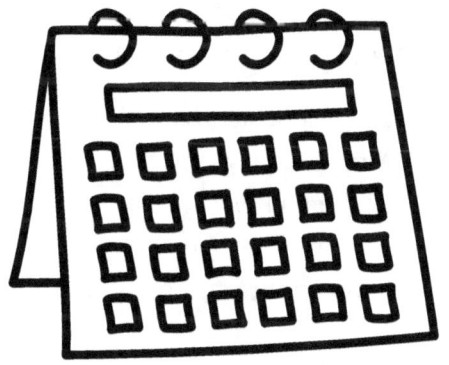

- **Emergency fund:** Needs to be very liquid. Keep it in a high-yield savings account so you can access it quickly in a real emergency, but not so quickly that you'll be tempted to spend it.
- **Short-term savings:** Goals within the next five years, like replacing your car, moving, a trip, or a down payment, also stay in savings, not investments.

3. RETIREMENT ACCOUNTS ARE NOT PIGGY BANKS

Money in your 401(k), 403(b), or Roth IRA is for your future self. Take money out early, and you'll pay taxes and penalties (unless it's Roth contributions; but even then, resist the urge). Once that money is gone, it's gone. And it misses years of growth.

The best move? Set it and forget it. Automate deposits, then stop checking the balance every week.

4. DON'T PANIC WHEN THE MARKET DROPS

If you look at your investments over just a year or two, it might seem like you've "lost" money. But those are on-paper losses; they only become real if you sell.

When the market dips, your shares drop in price, but you still own them. If you hold on, you'll still have them when prices recover.

> Rule: Any money you'll need within five years should stay in savings so you never have to sell investments at a loss.

CHAPTER 6 • INVEST

STARTING OUT: NOW & LATER

- **Now:** Build your emergency fund, pay off debt, and if possible, open a Roth IRA.
- **Later:** Keep 3–6 months of expenses in savings, then invest the rest in low-cost index funds.
- **Always:** Stay invested for the long term. Don't sell in downturns, and don't raid retirement accounts early.

PUTTING IT ALL TOGETHER

Investing is the final step in the personal finance system we've been building. It's the part that makes your money keep working for you, even after you stop working for it.

Here's the big picture: every dollar you invest now is buying back your future time. That's time you won't have to spend at a job you don't love, or working extra hours when you'd rather be traveling, starting your own business, or spending time with family.

YOUR STEP-BY-STEP GAME PLAN

1. **Know where you're starting.** Track how much money you earn, how much you spend, and how much debt (if any) you have.
2. **Increase your savings rate.** Earn more, spend less, and move money into savings as soon as you get paid so you're not tempted to spend it.
3. **Put your money to work.**
   - Build an emergency fund (6 months of expenses).
   - Pay off all debt.
   - Automate monthly investments into retirement and/or brokerage accounts.

WHY THIS WORKS AT ANY AGE

Whether you start in high school, college, or later, this is the same proven plan adults use to build wealth. It doesn't matter if it takes you two years or ten years to complete the steps as long as you keep moving forward, you will reach financial freedom.

Once your systems are running on autopilot, you'll have built something powerful: the ability to live life on your terms. That's when you can connect your money plan to your bigger life vision so the money you earn, save, and invest is actually creating the future you want. In the next chapter, we'll talk about how to design that vision and align it with your finances. Before you know it, you'll be living it and teaching others how they can do the same.

DEFINITIONS

You made it! Investing might not be the flashiest topic in this book, but now you've got the tools to run your money like a pro. Here's a quick recap of key terms from this chapter:

- **401(k) / 403(b)** – Retirement accounts you get through your job. Money goes in before taxes (so it lowers your taxable income now), but you'll pay taxes on it later when you withdraw it post-retirement. And if you withdraw it before retirement age, you may also get hit with a 10% penalty.
- **Brokerage account** – An account you open to buy and sell investments like stocks or index funds.
- **Brokerage firm** – The company where you keep your investment accounts. Popular options: Vanguard, Schwab, Fidelity.

- **Dividend** – A payout companies give to shareholders (a portion of the profits).
- **Index** – A "snapshot" of a part of the stock market, like the S&P 500 (the 500 biggest U.S. companies).
- **Index fund** – A type of mutual fund that invests in all the companies in a certain index. Example: VTSAX tracks the entire U.S. stock market.
- **IRA (Individual Retirement Account)** – A retirement account you open yourself (not through an employer). When you leave a job, you can "roll over" your 401(k)/403(b) into an IRA for more investment choices.
- **Liquidity** – How easily you can access your money. Checking accounts are very liquid. Retirement accounts are not.
- **Mutual fund** – A mix of many different stocks or bonds, all packaged together in one investment.
- **Roth IRA** – A retirement account where you put in after-tax money, and your investments grow tax-free. You can withdraw what you put in (but not the growth) at any time without penalty.
- **Stock** – A share of ownership in a company.
- **Stock market** – The place where stocks and other investments are bought and sold.

CHAPTER 6

Summary

- **Investing grows your money** so you can work less and live more in the future.

- **Save before you invest** – build an emergency fund and pay off debt first.

- **Match savings to your timeline** – keep short-term money in savings; invest only what you won't need for at least five years.

- **Protect your retirement accounts** – avoid early withdrawals to prevent penalties and lost growth.

- **Stay invested during market drops** – selling in a downturn locks in losses; let your investments recover.

- **Follow the 3-step plan** – know your finances, save more, and invest consistently in low-cost index funds.

CHAPTER 6
Reflection Questions

1. What comes to mind when you hear the word "investing"? Excitement? Fear? Confusion? Something else?

2. Have you seen anyone in your life model what it looks like to build wealth through investing? What did you learn from them?

3. If you could create a life where your money made money for you, what would that freedom allow you to do?

4. What questions do you still have about investing? How can you start finding the answers now?

5. If you were to start investing this month, even a small amount, what platform, index fund, or resource might you explore first?

6. How does learning to invest now change your timeline for financial freedom?

CHAPTER 7
Freedom

CHAPTER 7 • FREEDOM

We've covered a lot together in this book. You've learned how to avoid common money traps, break free from debt, and create space in your budget for something far better, financial freedom. You've built a vision for your future, found ways to earn more and spend less, and discovered how to grow your money through smart investing to create lasting wealth.

Now it's time for the final step: connecting your money plan to your life plan so you can live the freedom you've been working toward.

CHOOSE THE FREEDOM PATH THAT FITS YOU

Freedom looks different for everyone. For some, it's choosing where and how to work. For others, it's not working at all. You might not know yet which version fits you best, but you can start building toward either (or both) right now.

Here are the two main paths:

1. **Career Freedom** – This means having the money saved so you can walk away from a job that doesn't make you happy, take time off between jobs, or even start your own business without stressing about bills. Career Freedom lets you pick work you actually enjoy instead of feeling stuck in something you hate just because you need a paycheck.

2. **Total Freedom (aka Early Retirement)** – This is for people who want enough money invested so they never have to work for money again unless they *want* to. It's like hitting the pause button on the working world, permanently. Some people take this path so they can travel full-time, volunteer, focus on creative projects, or just relax and live life on their terms.

Here's the best part: You don't have to decide right now which one's for you. You can aim for one path, change your mind later, or even combine them. The key is to start building the habits that will give your future self the power to choose.

CREATING CAREER FREEDOM

Career Freedom is all about **options**. It means you've saved enough money to give yourself breathing room between jobs, say "no" to work you don't want, or take time to explore your own business ideas without worrying about how you'll pay the bills.

Imagine this: you graduate, land a decent job, and it's... fine. But after a year or two, you realize it's not what you want to do long-term. Most people feel trapped at this point because they need their paycheck to survive. But if you've been building a *Career Freedom Fund* from day one, you can step away, take a few months off, and focus on finding (or creating) work you're excited about without panicking about rent or food.

STEP 1: FIGURE OUT YOUR "FREEDOM NUMBER"

Your Freedom Number is the amount of money you'd need saved to live for a few months without income. For most people, 6 months' worth of bare bones living expenses is a good starting point.

Let's say your monthly costs look like the note on the next page.

That's $1,300/month. Multiply that by 6 months and your Freedom Number is **$7,800**. Once you've saved that, you officially have the power to leave a job or take a break without stressing about money.

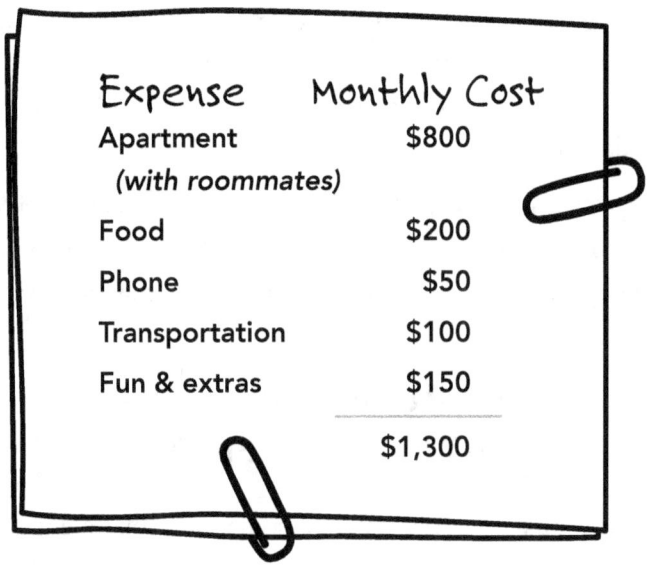

STEP 2: START SAVING AUTOMATICALLY

The easiest way to build this fund is to make it automatic:

- Open a separate savings account called "Freedom Fund."
- Have a set amount (even $25 or $50) automatically transferred every time you get paid from a job, side hustle, or allowance.
- Don't touch it unless you *really* need to take time off work or invest in your next career move.

STEP 3: USE IT STRATEGICALLY

Your Career Freedom Fund isn't for emergencies, it's for *opportunities.*

- Want to quit your part-time job to take an unpaid summer internship that will boost your career? You can.

- Need a few months to launch an online shop or tutoring business? You can.
- Want to move to a new city after college without a job lined up? You can.

When you know you could walk away from a job tomorrow and still be okay, you start making choices from a place of confidence, not fear. And that's the kind of freedom that changes everything.

WHY PLANNING BREAKS MATTERS, EVEN NOW

A lot of people think retirement is something you do once way off in the future. But there's another option: taking **mini-retirements** along the way.

A mini-retirement is simply a planned break from working so you can do something exciting, meaningful, or restorative without blowing up your long-term plans. Instead of waiting until you're 65 to live your dream life, you take chunks of it sooner.

For young people, this might sound like:

- Taking a gap year before or after college to travel, volunteer, or explore a passion project
- Spending a summer building a small business instead of working a regular job
- Traveling abroad for a few months after graduation to learn a language or immerse yourself in another culture

> These breaks work best when you **plan and save for them** in advance.

STEP 1: DECIDE WHAT YOU WANT TO DO

- Is your dream to travel to 5 different countries?
- Learn graphic design and build a portfolio?
- Work on a political campaign?
- Take a few months to focus on music, art, or writing?

Whatever it is, make it specific.

STEP 2: CREATE A BUDGET

Figure out how much it will cost. Include:

- Where you'll live (rent, hostels, staying with friends/family)
- Food and daily expenses
- Travel or program costs
- Health insurance if you'll be away from school or work

STEP 3: SAVE ON PURPOSE

- Open a separate "Break Fund" account
- Pick a savings target (even $3,000–$5,000 can fund a life-changing few months)
- Save a percentage of all your income from jobs, internships, or side hustles

STEP 4: MAKE IT HAPPEN

When the time comes, you won't be hesitating. You'll be ready. You'll have the money set aside, the plan in place, and the confidence to step away from work or school for a short time to do something extraordinary.

Why it matters now: When you're young, you don't have as many fixed expenses like a mortgage or kids, so taking breaks is easier and less risky. If you learn to plan and save for them now, you can keep taking them throughout your life without throwing your finances off track.

WHAT IS FINANCIAL FREEDOM – REALLY?

Earlier, I shared how I first stumbled onto the **FIRE** movement (**F**inancial **I**ndependence, **R**etire **E**arly) when I was looking for ways to save money. Now let's take a closer look at what that actually means.

At its core, financial freedom is having enough money saved and invested to live life completely on your own terms. For some people, that means never needing to work for money again. For others, it simply means having the option to stop whenever they want.

The exciting part? You don't have to win the lottery, build a million-dollar business overnight, or land a high-paying job to get there. The formula is simple: save, invest, and let time do the heavy lifting.

CHAPTER 7 • FREEDOM

THE 4% RULE (MADE SIMPLE)

Here's the math behind FIRE:

- If you invest enough money, you can safely take out about **4% of it every year** for the rest of your life.
- Your investments will keep growing in the background, replacing what you spend.

Think of it like planting a giant money tree: each year you can pick some fruit (spend money), but the tree keeps growing new fruit at the same pace, so it never runs out.

YOUR RETIREMENT NUMBER

Your *retirement number* is how much money you need invested so that 4% covers your yearly expenses.

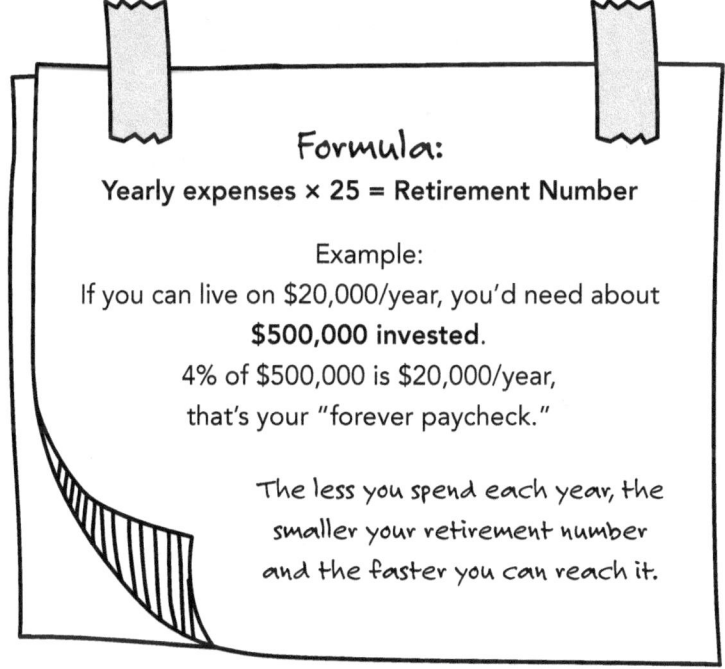

Formula:
Yearly expenses × 25 = Retirement Number

Example:
If you can live on $20,000/year, you'd need about **$500,000 invested**.
4% of $500,000 is $20,000/year,
that's your "forever paycheck."

The less you spend each year, the smaller your retirement number and the faster you can reach it.

WHY YOU HAVE A HUGE ADVANTAGE RIGHT NOW

Here's why being young is your secret weapon: **time**.

- If you start investing as a young person, even small amounts grow into massive numbers thanks to compound interest (interest earning interest).
- Starting early means you can save less each month but still end up with more than someone who starts 10 years later.
- Invest $100/month from age 18–28 → stop adding money → over $75,000 by age 50.
- Wait until age 28 to start and invest $100/month until age 50 → less than $60,000.

That's the power of starting now, even with small amounts.

FIND YOUR FIRE

Now that you know how financial independence works, the next step is to decide **how fast** you want to get there and **what life will look like** along the way. There's no single path, just the one that fits *your* goals, personality, and lifestyle.

Here are three of the most popular approaches to FIRE, reimagined for where you are now:

1. FAST-TRACK FIRE (AKA LEAN FIRE)

This is for people who want financial independence *as soon as possible*. They're willing to live super frugally, spending the bare minimum, so they can save and invest the maximum.

What this might look like for you in your early career:

- Living with roommates or at home to save on rent
- Biking or using public transportation instead of owning a car
- Working multiple jobs or a job plus a side hustle
- Putting 60–70% of your income into investments

> **The trade-off:** You get to financial independence quickly, but you'll need to be okay with a simpler lifestyle, both now and in retirement.

2. BALANCED FIRE (AKA SLOW FIRE)

This is for people who want to enjoy life now *and* later. Instead of going to extremes, they save and invest consistently while still spending on things they value.

What this might look like for you:

- Saving 30–50% of your income while budgeting for travel, concerts, or hobbies
- Splurging on experiences or items that bring joy, but skipping the stuff you don't care about
- Planning for financial independence in 15–20 years instead of 5–10

> **The trade-off:** It takes longer to reach financial independence, but you're living a life you enjoy along the way.

The Power of Compound Interest

Jalisa
- Starts investing at age 25
- Invests $20,000 every year for 10 years
- No investments after age 34
- Total investment: **$200,000**
- Total at age 65: **$2,103,487**

Josh
- Starts investing at age 35
- Invests $20,000 every year for 30 years
- Total investment: **$600,000**
- Total at age 65: **$1,889,216**

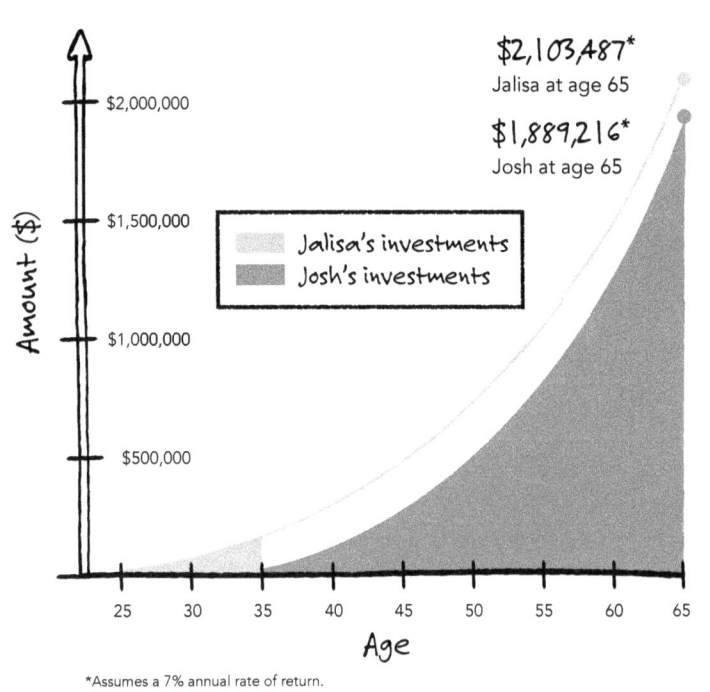

*Assumes a 7% annual rate of return.

3. SET-IT-AND-FORGET-IT FIRE (AKA COAST FIRE)

Perfect for people starting early (like you) who want to front-load their investing. You invest heavily in your first few working years, then let compound interest carry you the rest of the way.

What this might look like:

- Saving and investing 50%+ of your income in your first 5–10 years of work
- Keeping your expenses low while you're young (roommates, modest lifestyle)
- Knowing that even if you never invest another dollar, your early savings will grow enough to fund your retirement

The trade-off: You work now to invest a lot early, but later in life, you can relax your savings rate because your money is already working for you.

WHICH PATH IS RIGHT FOR YOU?

Think about:

- How quickly you want financial freedom
- Whether you're okay with frugal living or prefer more balance
- What you value most right now vs. later

You can even mix and match, starting with Fast-Track FIRE for a few years, then switching to Balanced or Set-It-and-Forget-It FIRE.

Remember: The goal isn't to follow someone else's plan, it's to design a money strategy that gives <u>you</u> the life you want.

YOUR MOVE: START BUILDING FREEDOM NOW

You've just learned that financial freedom isn't one-size-fits-all. You get to decide how fast you want to get there, what the journey looks like, and what kind of life you'll live when you arrive.

The most important thing to remember is this: **your biggest advantage is starting early.** You have decades ahead for your money to grow, and the choices you make now can completely change your future.

Here's your challenge:

1. **Run your numbers** – Figure out your Freedom Number and how much you'd need to invest to hit it.
2. **Pick your FIRE style** – Fast-Track, Balanced, or Set-It-and-Forget-It.
3. **Start today** – Even if it's just transferring $10 or $25 into a savings or investment account, take the first step.

> Every dollar you save and invest now is buying your future self more choices, more time, and more freedom. Don't wait for "someday." Start building your dream life today because the sooner you begin, the sooner you'll have the power to live it.

Design a **money plan** that gives you the life you want.

CHAPTER 7
Summary

- **Two paths to freedom** – Career Freedom (money saved to give you job choices) and Total Freedom/Early Retirement (enough invested to never have to work for money again).
- **Career Freedom starts with your Freedom Number** – Calculate 6 months of living expenses, save it in a separate account, and use it for opportunities.
- **Mini-retirements give you breaks along the way** – Plan ahead with a clear goal, budget, and savings target for travel, projects, or learning experiences.
- **The 4% Rule is your roadmap** – You can safely spend 4% of your investments each year forever. Your Retirement Number = yearly expenses × 25.
- **Lower spending means a lower goal** – The less you need to live on, the faster you can reach financial independence.
- **Starting early is your superpower** – Small amounts invested young grow far more over time than larger amounts started later.
- **Three FIRE paths fit different lifestyles:**
  - Fast-Track FIRE – Save 60–70% of your income for the quickest independence.
  - Balanced FIRE – Save 30–50%, enjoy life along the way.
  - Set-It-and-Forget-It FIRE – Invest heavily for 5–10 years, then let compound interest do the rest.
- **Action steps** – Pick your FIRE style, calculate your Freedom Number, and start saving and investing today, no matter the amount.

CHAPTER 7
Reflection Questions

1. What does freedom mean to you, in your own words?

2. Can you think of a time when money (or the lack of it) limited your choices? How did that experience impact you?

3. How would your daily life look different if money were no longer a constant concern?

4. What financial habits or mindsets could help you feel more free, even before you reach your ultimate goals?

5. What's one financial boundary you want to start holding or reinforcing to protect your peace and purpose?

6. What does your financial freedom journey look like over the next 5 years? What steps will get you there?

Conclusion

CONCLUSION

If you've made it to the end of this book, let me say this first: I'm proud of you. Most people go their whole lives never learning how money really works. But you? You're starting early. You're making moves. You're taking your future seriously. That already puts you ahead of the game.

Now here's the truth: You don't have to be a genius, a straight-A student, or a future millionaire to build wealth. You just have to make a different set of choices than most people do. While others are signing up for debt, chasing trends, or hoping things magically work out, you'll be creating a plan and building real freedom one smart step at a time.

Freedom isn't just about money. It's about waking up and deciding how you want to spend your time. It's about being able to say "no" to things that drain you and "yes" to opportunities that excite you. It's about taking care of your people, your mental health, and your goals without being held back by money stress.

And you don't have to wait until "someday" to feel that kind of freedom.

You can start now.
You can build your emergency fund.
You can skip the debt traps.
You can earn more, spend smart, and invest early.
You can design a life you actually want.

You have the power to create a future where money gives you options instead of limits. And the best part? When you get free, you make it easier for other people around you to get free too.

So go ahead. Dream big, stay focused, and take that next step. You've got this.

Glossary

CREDIT & DEBT

- **AnnualCreditReport.com** – The official website where you can get a free copy of your credit report from each of the three major credit bureaus once per year.
- **Credit Report** – A record of your borrowing history, including loans, credit cards, and payment patterns. Lenders use it to decide whether to give you credit.
- **Credit Score** – A number that shows how reliable you are at borrowing and paying back money. A higher score makes it easier to get loans and credit cards.
- **Credit Utilization Ratio** – The percentage of your available credit limit you're using. A lower ratio can help your credit score.
- **Debt** – Money you owe to someone else, like a loan, mortgage, or credit card balance.
- **Equifax** – One of the three main credit reporting companies in the U.S. that compiles credit reports.
- **Experian** – One of the three main credit reporting companies in the U.S. that compiles credit reports.
- **Forbearance** – A temporary pause or reduction in loan payments, during which interest may still accrue.
- **Interest** – The cost of borrowing money, shown as a percentage of the amount you owe. Interest can also work in your favor when you earn it on savings or investments.
- **Principal** – The original amount of money borrowed on a loan or the amount still owed, not counting interest.
- **TransUnion** – One of the three main credit reporting companies in the U.S. that compiles credit reports.

CAR BUYING

- **Carfax** – A service that provides a car's history report, including accidents, ownership, and service records.
- **Carvana** – An online car-buying service where you can shop, finance, and arrange delivery of a vehicle.
- **Certified Pre-Owned** – A used car that has passed an inspection and meets specific manufacturer standards, often including a warranty.
- **Dealerships** – Businesses that sell new and/or used cars, often offering financing and warranties.
- **Enterprise Car Sales** – A car sales program from Enterprise Rent-A-Car that offers used cars for sale, often with warranties.
- **Kelley Blue Book** – A trusted guide for finding a car's market value.
- **Microwave Method** – A quick approach to getting a car, often by financing immediately instead of saving up; usually more expensive over time.
- **Private Sellers** – Individuals who sell their own cars directly to buyers without going through a dealership.
- **Slow-Cooker Method** – A patient approach to buying a car by saving up cash over time, starting with a cheaper vehicle and upgrading gradually.

EDUCATION & SCHOLARSHIPS

- **100% of Demonstrated Financial Need** – When a college covers the full gap between your family's ability to pay and the school's cost, based on financial aid formulas.
- **Academic Scholarships** – Awards based on grades, test scores, or other academic achievements.
- **AmeriCorps** – A national service program where you work on community projects in exchange for a living allowance and education award.
- **Athletic and Music Scholarships** – Awards based on skill in sports or music, often requiring participation on a team or in a program.
- **Free Application for Federal Student Aid (FAFSA)** – A form that determines eligibility for federal, state, and school-based financial aid for college.
- **In-State Tuition** – A lower tuition rate for students who live in the same state as a public college or university.
- **Local and Regional Scholarships** – Awards offered by community organizations, businesses, or foundations in your city or state.
- **Pell Grant** – Federal grant money for college students with financial need that does not have to be repaid.

REAL ESTATE & LIFESTYLE

- **Geo-Arbitrage** – Earning money in a high-paying location but living or spending in a lower-cost area to maximize savings.
- **House Hacking** – A strategy where you live in one part of a property and rent out the rest to help cover your housing costs.
- **Slow Flips** – Buying a property, living in it while making gradual improvements, and then selling it for a profit.

INVESTING

- **Automatic Transfers** – Setting up your bank account or paycheck to move money into savings or investment accounts on a set schedule.
- **Bond** – A type of investment where you loan money to a government or company, and they pay you back with interest.
- **Brokerage Account** – An account you open to buy and sell investments like stocks, bonds, or index funds.
- **Brokerage Firm** – The company where you keep your investment accounts. Popular options include Vanguard, Schwab, and Fidelity.
- **Capitalist Economy** – An economic system where businesses and individuals own resources, and goods and services are produced for profit.
- **Compound Interest** – Interest earned on both the money you invest and the interest it has already earned.
- **Custodial Investment Account** – An account opened by an adult for a minor to invest money, managed by the adult until the child reaches legal age.

GLOSSARY

- **Diversification** – Spreading your investments across different types of assets to reduce risk.
- **Dividend** – A payout companies give to shareholders, usually a portion of their profits.
- **ETF (Exchange-Traded Fund)** – A basket of investments, like stocks or bonds, that you can buy and sell on the stock market just like a single stock.
- **Employer Match** – When your employer adds extra money to your retirement account based on how much you contribute.
- **Index** – A "snapshot" of part of the stock market, like the S&P 500 (the 500 biggest U.S. companies).
- **Index Fund** – A type of mutual fund that invests in all the companies in a certain index. Example: VTSAX tracks the entire U.S. stock market.
- **Investment** – Something you buy or put money into because you expect it to grow in value or earn income over time.
- **Investment Accounts** – Accounts where you hold and manage investments like stocks, bonds, or funds.
- **Mutual Fund** – A mix of many different stocks or bonds, all packaged together in one investment.
- **Stock** – A share of ownership in a company. When you own a stock, you own a piece of that company.
- **Stock Market** – The place where people buy and sell shares (stocks) of companies and other investments.
- **Tax Benefits** – Ways the government reduces your taxes if you save or invest in certain accounts, like retirement plans.
- **VTI (Vanguard Total Stock Market ETF)** – A popular Vanguard ETF that lets you invest in almost the entire U.S. stock market at once.
- **VTSAX** – A mutual fund from Vanguard that tracks the entire U.S. stock market.

GLOSSARY

FINANCIAL INDEPENDENCE & PLANNING

- **401(k) / 403(b)** – Retirement accounts you get through your job. Money goes in before taxes (so it lowers your taxable income now), but you'll pay taxes later on and you may also pay a 10% penalty if you withdraw money before retirement age.
- **4% Rule** – A guideline for early retirement. If you invest enough money, you can withdraw 4% of it each year and have it last forever because your investments keep growing in the background.
- **Annual Expenses** – The total amount of money you spend in a year. Used to calculate your Retirement Number.
- **Asset** – Something valuable you own, like cash, investments, or a house. Assets can grow in value or help you make money.
- **Balanced FIRE (Slow FIRE)** – A path to financial independence that balances saving with enjoying life now.
- **Career Freedom** – Having enough savings to leave a job, take time off, or explore new opportunities without stressing about money.
- **Set-It-and-Forget-It FIRE (Coast FIRE)** – Reaching a point where you've invested enough early that your money will grow on its own to fund your retirement, even if you stop investing more.
- **Emergency Fund** – Money set aside for unexpected expenses, like car repairs or medical bills.
- **Fast-Track FIRE (Lean FIRE)** – A path to financial independence that focuses on extreme saving and frugality to reach the goal as quickly as possible.
- **Financial Independence** – When you have enough money saved and invested that you no longer need to work for a paycheck.

GLOSSARY

- **FIRE (Financial Independence, Retire Early)** – A movement of people who save and invest aggressively to reach financial independence decades before traditional retirement age.
- **Freedom Fund** – A savings account that gives you options, such as quitting a job, taking a break, or starting a business without worrying about money.
- **Income** – Money you earn from work, investments, or other sources.
- **Inflation** – The rise in prices over time, which means your money buys less in the future.
- **IRA (Individual Retirement Account)** – A retirement account you open yourself, not through an employer. You can "roll over" an old 401(k) or 403(b) into an IRA for more investment choices.
- **Liquidity** – How easily you can access your money. Checking accounts are very liquid; retirement accounts are not.
- **Mini-Retirement** – A planned break from work to travel, learn, volunteer, or explore passions before traditional retirement age.
- **Retirement Number** – The total amount you need invested to cover your annual expenses using the 4% rule.
- **Roth IRA** – A retirement account where you put in after-tax money and your investments grow tax-free. You can withdraw what you put in (but not the growth) at any time without penalty.
- **Savings Rate** – The percentage of your income you save or invest instead of spending.
- **Side Hustle** – Extra work you do outside your main job to earn more money.
- **Total Freedom (Early Retirement)** – Having enough invested so you never have to work for money again unless you choose to.

Index

INDEX

A

Academic scholarships, 61
After-tax money, 126, 133
Alumni network, 104
AmeriCorps, 63, 65
Athletic and music scholarships, 62
Available credit, 24, 28
Average growth, 125

B

Balance, 22–25, 31–33, 36, 41–42, 68, 72, 130, 147
Big expenses, 108–109, 116
Budget, 29, 33, 44, 47, 63, 65, 111, 113, 116, 119, 137, 141, 150
Budgeting, 111–114, 145
Budgeting apps, 113

C

Cable, 107 108, 119
Capitalist economy, 120
Car depreciation, 41–42
Car insurance, 29, 36, 108, 111
Car payment, 43–45, 50–51, 107
Career freedom, 137–139, 150
Carfax, 46–47, 50
Carvana, 50
Cell phone plans, 108
Certified pre-owned, 156
Coca-Cola Scholars, 61
Coding, 55, 101, 103
Compound interest, 22, 25, 144, 146–147, 150
Core value, 81
Cover letter, 105
Creativity, 81
Creator, 84

Credentials, 55, 57, 70
Credit cards, 15–16, 22, 25, 33, 36–37, 53, 59, 67, 72–73
Credit history, length of, 28
Credit mix, 28–29
Credit report, 24, 29
Credit scores, 29, 32, 36
Credit utilization ratio, 28
Custodial account, 125

D

Dealership, 41, 46, 50
Debt, struggle with, 22
Debt treadmill, 32
Deductible, 108
Definition of:
  Brokerage account, 127–128, 131–132
  Brokerage firm, 133
  Dividend, 122, 133
  401(k) / 403(b), 132
  Index, 120–125, 127, 131–135
  Index fund, 135
  IRA, 130–131, 133
  Liquidity, 128, 133
  Mutual fund, 133
  Roth IRA, 130–131, 133
  Stock, 132–133
  Stock market, 125, 133
Digital marketing, 103
Discover what you like, 81
Dreaming big, 79

E

Early jobs, 103
Emergency fund, 22–23, 30, 32, 36–37, 114, 128, 130–131, 134
Employer match, 127–128

Enterprise Car Sales, 46
Equifax, 29
Experian, 29, 44

F

Fast-track FIRE, 144, 150
Federal grant money, 157
Fellowships, 106
Fidelity 500 Index Fund (FXAIX), 125
Financial freedom, 16, 20, 22, 24, 122, 126, 128, 130, 132, 135, 137–138, 146–148, 151
Financial need, 62
Financing, 34, 36, 41, 47, 50
Fire, approaches to:
Balanced FIRE (aka Slow FIRE), 145, 150
Fast-track FIRE (aka Lean FIRE), 144, 150
Set-it-and-forget-it FIRE (aka Coast FIRE), 147, 150
FIRE movement, 119, 142
First full-time role, 114
Forbearance, 59, 68
4% rule, 143, 150
Free Application for Federal Student Aid (FAFSA), 62, 64–65
Freedom, budget for, 111
Freedom number, 138, 148, 150
Freelance work, 103
Funding sources, 61, 64

G

Gates Foundation, 61
Geo-arbitrage, 109
Grants, 60, 62, 64–65, 67, 106

H

Hard inquiry, 25
High-interest debt, 73, 128
House hacking, 109
Housing, 29, 107, 109, 116, 122

I

Ideal day, 78, 86, 97
Index funds, 120–125, 131–132, 134
Inflation, 122
In-state tuition, 63, 65
Interest, 22–25, 27–30, 47–48, 72–73, 102, 128, 144, 146–147, 150
Interest rates, 24, 28, 34, 47, 56
Investing, 50, 109, 114, 127–135, 137, 144, 146–147, 150
Investing, start as young person, 144
Investment accounts, 123, 133

J

Jack Kent Cooke Foundation, 63
Jackie Robinson Foundation, 61
Job loss, 22, 30, 36

K

Kelley Blue Book, 41, 46, 50

L

Late payments, 24
Lifetime investing order, 127
LinkedIn profile, 105
Liquidity, 128, 133
Loan balance, 41–42
Loan trap, 59

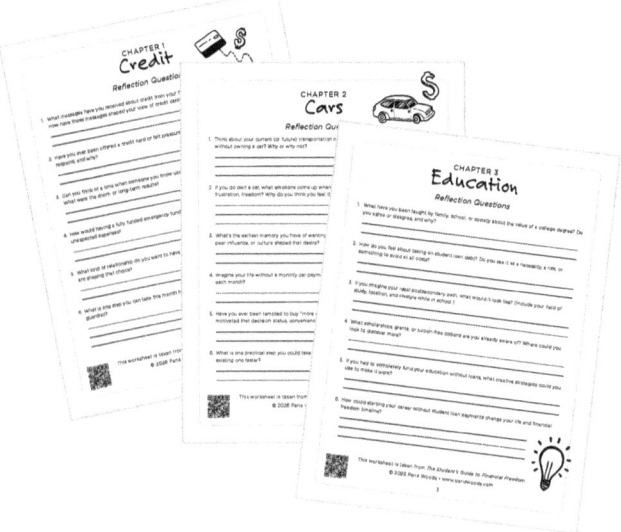

Get the
PRINTABLE VERSIONS
of every exercise in this book at
pariswoods.com/students

Connect

Did this book help you see money differently?
Here's how to keep the momentum going:

LEAVE A REVIEW ON AMAZON.

Your feedback helps other students, parents, and educators find this book. Even a short one-line review makes a difference.

FOLLOW ME ON SOCIAL MEDIA.

Stay inspired with quick tips, tools, and real-life money strategies. You'll also be the first to know about new resources, courses, and opportunities.

Follow me on Instagram, TikTok, and YouTube:
@authorpariswoods

SHARE THIS BOOK.

If you have a friend, sibling, or classmate who could benefit from this information, pass it along. You could change their future.

ABOUT THE AUTHOR

Dr. **Paris Woods** is a first-generation college graduate who earned her bachelor's degree from Harvard College without taking on student debt. She later earned a master's degree from Harvard and a doctorate from The University of Texas at Austin, building a career dedicated to helping others achieve education and financial freedom.

Paris began her career as an admissions and financial aid officer at Harvard, where she helped students navigate college access and affordability. She also served as a certified tax preparer through the IRS Volunteer Income Tax Assistance (VITA) program, supporting individuals and families in making informed financial decisions.

An award-winning education leader and bestselling author, Paris has helped thousands of people learn to take control of their money, build wealth, and design the life they want. Her first book, *The Black Girl's Guide to Financial Freedom*, has sold over 100,000 copies and been praised by leading financial experts for its clear, practical advice. She also co-founded College Beyond, a nonprofit supporting students on the path to college graduation and career success.

Paris is passionate about giving young people the knowledge and tools to start early and dream big, because starting early changes everything. When she's not writing or speaking, she enjoys exploring new cities, listening to live music, and working toward her goal of visiting all seven continents.

About the Author

Slow flips, 109
Slow-cooker method, 48, 50
Stackable scholarships, 106
Streaming, 107–108

T

Target date fund, 127
Tax-free, 126, 133
Technology, 107
Total freedom, 137, 150
Tracking method, 113
Transferable skills, 105
Transportation, 40, 51, 107–108, 116–117, 119, 145
TransUnion, 29
Travel, 16, 50, 81, 83, 109, 112, 120, 137, 141, 145
Two golden rules for smart car ownership, 50

U

Unexpected bills, 30
United Negro College Fund, 61
Utilities, 30, 107–109, 111, 113

V

Vanguard Total Stock Market ETF (VTI), 122, 125
Vanguard Total Stock Market Index Fund (VTSAX), 122, 133
Video editing, 103
Vision, 77–78, 81–83, 91, 96–97, 132, 137

W

Work-study, 60, 111, 114

P

Paid internships, 103
Part-time job, 31, 60, 63, 102, 104–105, 111, 114, 139
Pay in full, 28, 31, 36
Pay minimum only, 27
Payment history, 28–29
Payment plan, 22, 59, 63, 65, 68
Pell Grant, 62, 65
Postsecondary, 53, 55, 57, 59, 70–71
Postsecondary education, 53, 57
Principal, 25
Private sellers, 46, 50
Private university, 60
Professional experience, 102–103

R

Raise, 106–107
Regular brokerage account, 127–128
Resident advisor, 109
Résumé, 101, 104–105, 116–117
Retirement accounts, 130–134
Retirement number, 143, 150
Roommates, 31, 109, 139, 145, 147
Roth IRA (Individual Retirement Account), 123, 126–127, 130–131, 133

S

Salary, 57, 59, 68, 101, 106–107
Saving vs. investing, 128
Scholarships, 60–65, 67, 103, 106
Schwab Total Stock Market Index Fund (SWTSX), 125
Secondary education, 54–55
Separate bank accounts, 113 Short-term savings, 130
Side hustles, 103, 141
Simple investment strategy, 119

Loans, 15–16, 22, 24, 28–29, 56–57, 59, 63, 65, 67–73
Local and regional scholarships, 63
Long-term payments, 30
Low-cost index funds, 120, 131
Lower-interest debt, 73
Low-income, 61–62, 64–65
Low-income families, students from, 62

M

Medical issues, 30
Microwave method, 48
Middle-income, 61, 64–65
Milestones, 114, 116
Mini-experiments, 83, 92
Minimum payment trap, 25
Mini-retirements, 140, 150
Money trap, 50, 72, 137
Motivation, 80, 84, 100, 114
Moving costs, 30

N

National Merit Scholarship Corporation, 61
Net price, 60, 62, 64
Networking, 101–102, 104–105, 116–117
New credit, 21, 28
Notes app method, 113

O

100% of demonstrated financial need, 62
Online courses, 102–103
Online presence, 106, 117
Online profiles, 105

www.ingramcontent.com/pod-product-compliance
Lightning Source LLC
LaVergne TN
LVHW021719060526
838200LV00050B/2746